# Leadership & Lincoln:
## 100 Principles and Practices Drawn from the President's Words

## Greg M. Romaneck

"With malice toward none; with charity for all"

(A. Lincoln)

"Leadership & Lincoln," by Greg M. Romaneck. ISBN 1-58939-974-9.

Published 2006 by Virtualbookworm.com Publishing Inc., P.O. Box 9949, College Station, TX 77842, US. ©2006, Greg Romaneck. All rights reserved. No part of this publication may be reproduced, stored in a retrieval system, or transmitted in any form or by any means, electronic, mechanical, recording or otherwise, without the prior written permission of Greg M. Romaneck.

Manufactured in the United States of America.

# Leadership & Lincoln:
## 100 Principles and Practices Drawn from the President's Words

# Introduction

A braham Lincoln remains one of the iconic figures in American history. Born in a backwoods cabin in Kentucky Abe Lincoln came into a world that could little guess what heights he would rise to. Lincoln's boyhood in rural Kentucky and Indiana was marked by loss and want. The untimely death of his mother after the family had moved to southern Indiana left young Abe in the charge of his disengaged father. Fortunately young Lincoln was to fall under the tutelage of a loving stepmother who helped him overcome what could have been a devastating turn of events. Over time, young Mr. Lincoln moved to Illinois where he worked hard to establish himself as a man of value. In the end, Lincoln's hard work, intuitive mind, common sense, and amazing talent for getting to the heart of people stood him in good stead.

Many Americans have no idea how often Abe Lincoln experienced defeat and loss in his life. To the majority of modern Americans Lincoln is a mythical figure who lived, died, and left a legacy of near sainthood. In reality, Abraham Lincoln went through trials and tribulations that could easily have blunted the edge of his wit and wisdom. Within his family Abe Lincoln lived to see the death of his mother, two sons, his rejected father, and thousands of innocent citizens who he was responsible for sending off to war. In addition, Mr. Lincoln was married to a woman, Mary Todd, whom he loved but who also carried with her a great deal of emotional baggage. Known as "the hellcat" by one of Lincoln's minions, Mary Todd Lincoln cost her husband a great deal of energy and thought.

Politically, Abraham Lincoln's career was anything but seamless. In his day Mr. Lincoln lost or was excluded from elections for positions including state representative, congressman, and senator. Many people remember events such as the Lincoln-Douglas debates but fail to realize that Abraham

Lincoln lost that campaign. Even Mr. Lincoln's first presidential victory encompassed a minority of votes cast. All in all, it could be said that Abraham Lincoln did not possess an unblemished record of political victories. Given these factors how was Mr. Lincoln able to persevere and rise to the apex of leadership in America? Further, how did Abraham Lincoln cope with the arduous demands that his time in office made upon him?

Abe Lincoln presided over the most tumultuous and compelling era in American history. During his time in the White House over 630,000 Americans died in the Civil War. Invading armies devastated a large swathe of the nation. Grief and anger swept across the land. For a very long time it seemed that the mighty forces of the Union would lose the war for reasons that centered upon poor leadership. Yet, throughout all of this discord, Abraham Lincoln was able to cope with the demands of office and overcome obstacles that should have crushed him. How was that possible?

In looking at the thoughts of Abraham Lincoln as expressed in his words and writings modern day leaders can come away with a bounty of information. Lincoln led his nation at its darkest hour. Americans who presently embrace fear and anger over events such as the tragic 9/11 terrorist attacks would do well to stop and think about the devastation and despair that the Civil War bred. Across four long years Americans slaughtered one another in an appalling way. Brother fought against brother and Abraham Lincoln had to face the grim arithmetic of those losses on a daily basis. Thus, through the thoughts of this great leader we can come away with a deeper understanding not only of the way in which Mr. Lincoln worked but also how we can operate as leaders as well. Hopefully, in looking at the words of Mr. Lincoln, and the interpretive essays that are attached to each quotation in this slim volume, a modern day reader can reflect upon the lessons offered by this classic leader.

In closing I offer you the following thoughts about how this book is organized. Each of the 100 selections that follow is set up in a uniform manner. A quote from Mr. Lincoln appears at the top of the page in bold face. A brief reflective selection dealing with a related concept in leadership follows that quotation. It is hoped that the combination of Mr. Lincoln's thoughts, with a modern day application of them, will be of value to the reader. The text of this book is set out in such a way that the reader can select any one of the 100 entries at their pleasure, read the book from front to rear in one sitting, or take the selections one at a time over the course of the year. That decision is purely in the hands of the reader. I wish you the best of fortune in your study of leadership and perhaps, through the words of Abraham Lincoln, you can be moved to engage in a reflective look at how you function in your roles at work and in life.

# Dedication

This book is dedicated to my family. Without their support I could not have accomplished much of what I have done. It is in the family that the greatest love, inspiration, and compassion reside. Thanks and affection to each of you and please realize how much I care about you. GMR

# 1

## *"True patriotism is more holy than false piety"*

**B**EING A LEADER CAN BE A VERY DAUNTING TASK. YOU WILL BE bombarded with needs, demands, questions, and concerns on a daily basis. The way in which you make decisions, as much as the decisions you make, will define the reputation or image you establish. However, reputation is merely an external definition of who and what you are. The true measure of a person is what their character and values are. Your core beliefs, and the actions that flow out of them, will truly be your measure. The image that you try to project or that others interpret is an external process. Growth and service flow out of your internal processes and the way they, in turn, connect with others. Remember, you are what you think and the actions you take. Striving for fame, repute, or notice may be appropriate but they are not processes that will help either you or others in the long run.

# 2

## *"The dogmas of the quiet past are inadequate to the stormy present...as our case is new, so we must think anew and act anew."*

**C**HANGE CAN BE ONE OF THE MOST FRIGHTENING ASPECTS OF existence. People become comfortable and content with the status quo. However, the thought that things are remaining the same is a fallacy. Even as you read these lines everything in the world is in motion or flux. Change is an inherent part of life. Even down to the atomic or cellular level we are constantly reshaping ourselves. Thus, the commonly held belief that an innovation, crisis, or alteration of your circumstances is by definition hostile is probably at least an exaggeration. Change in normal times can be taxing but when unusual circumstances arise it may be wrenching. Faced with crisis or enforced change people can fall back upon past practices and wishes in order to try to pull themselves through. Yet, to simply rely on the dogmas or patterns of behavior of the past may be a faulty strategy. If you are faced with unforeseen or sweeping changes in your life you will be stressed. Yet, to try to hope that things will return to what they once were is a reasonably surefire pathway to despair. The world is what it is. To struggle against inevitabilities or to dream of what you wish things were like is to ignore reality. In such situations you need to at least try to see positive outcomes and attempt to adapt to new circumstances. New situations may result in unforeseen growth and development. At the very least, by trying to rethink the new situation you open the door to contentment that will not occur if you struggle against reality and attempt to recreate a passing dream world. Look change in the eye and acknowledge that, even though the situation is flawed, you will think creatively to do your best and live the best way you can.

2

# 3

## *"Tact is the ability to see others as they see themselves."*

SOME PEOPLE FEEL COMPELLED TO JUDGE THE BEHAVIOR OF others. They see the faults in everyone around them and are more than willing to share their opinions. The rush to judgment is a trait that many people possess. Yet, is judging another person and finding them deficient a pathway to growth? Or, on the other hand, is criticism a vehicle for helping people to progress? Perhaps the keynote point when offering criticism is to look at the situation in a unique way. Every person brings some strengths to the table. In a given situation those strengths may not be in use or the circumstance may be such that the person is not doing well. In such situations constructive criticism and feedback is a leadership responsibility. However, such positive criticism should not be confused with personal judgment or attack. In giving performance feedback a leader must be fair and objective while also balancing the needs of the person involved. Criticism cannot be personal in nature or destructive. Critical feedback should be delivered with an eye toward growth and not punishment. Even in extreme situations where the person in question is negative and hurtful to others the tone of your feedback must be professional in nature and comprehensive in scope. We, as leaders, do no one any favors when we look away from problems that have to be dealt with. Similarly, if we use vindictive or attacking tactics in giving criticism to others we are no longer leaders but rather bullies. At the heart of the matter rests the intent of your criticism. Is it aimed at performance and not the person? Are you offering suggestions that could remediate the problem? Are you being fair and objective in your feedback? If the answer to these interrogatories is "yes" then you are working from a corrective feedback framework. If the answers are "no" then reflect on what you are doing and how you should proceed.

# 4

## *"Inequality is certainly never to be embraced for its own sake."*

THE ISSUE OF CONTROL IS A MAJOR ONE FOR ALL TOO MANY leaders. It is easy to don a mantle of power and believe that, by virtue of your position, you are in control of everything and anything around you. In some cases personality traits in leaders include dominance as a touchstone point. Sadly, the more a person struggles to exert control over others the less real power they wield. Yes, a threatening or menacing boss can quell opposition by the strength of his or her bullying but is that really healthy for any organization? Those people who feel they must control or dominate a situation will generally fail over time. In history, no dictatorship has survived eternally. Likewise, in organizations overt and covert rebellion will result if the boss feels that he or she must dominate everything. Simply put, we control very little in life and when we think we are in control we may be deceiving ourselves. Given this reality, humbly acknowledging our limitations might be a better track to follow. Progress generally occurs through the actions of groups of people and not individuals. Yes, there are amazing leaders who by virtue of their exceptional ability, charisma, and knowledge can lift an organization up onto their back and move it along, but this is a rare circumstance indeed. More typically, a leader who more realistically acknowledges the things that they can and cannot control, or who does not see control as a driving factor in their life, will achieve more than a patent bully. Through the acknowledgement of what can be accomplished and then working with others to accomplish positive goals lies success. Rarely will success come from forcing the brunt of your will into the lives of others. As the renowned management guru Ken Blanchard says, "None of us is as smart as all of us."

# 5

## *"We dare not disregard the lessons of experience."*

H OW OFTEN HAVE YOU COME ACROSS A PERSON WHO IS SO BENT upon their own ideas that they fail to take heed of any advice or historical data? Unfortunately, it is all too frequent for people to fail to take heed of the lessons of the past while planning for the future. The simple fact is that every action or reaction is connected to a whole series of idiosyncratic events in a person's life. When we make decisions we do so based upon a pattern of decision making and concomitant successes or failures that have marked our life. Each person is a product of the environment and innate factors that went into their own creation. We do not function in a vacuum nor are we isolated bits of matter floating along in time. We are social beings who function in the real world of competing variables. Each choice we are confronted with or given the rare opportunity to make has not come out of nowhere. One of the gravest mistakes that a leader can make is to ignore history. We live in the present moment but are all too often thinking about past and future concerns. In order to appreciate where we are and get where we should be it is incumbent upon a thoughtful leader to bear witness to the past. History does not bind us. We can overcome the forces of history, past practice, and habituation but only if we thoughtfully understand what has come before. Just as Abraham Lincoln could not ignore the events that led to the crisis of the Civil War neither can any other leader scoff at historical variables that exist and continue to shape current practices. Effective leaders are historians or know who the historians are in their organization and what their expertise is.

## 6

## *"The loss of enemies does not compensate for the loss of friends."*

IT IS AN OLD QUESTION AS TO WHETHER OR NOT THE ENDS JUSTIFY the means? In the world of work rarely is a result worth any cost. If you go to war over a given issue without realizing the full cost of such action you are behaving in the most careless manner. Yes, there are huge issues of principles, morals, and ethics that require firmness of purpose. In a leader's career he or she will face such issues and must be prepared to act in a professional and strong manner. Yet, it is an unfortunate truth that all too many supervisors pick far too many battles that gradually ebb away both strength and credibility. It is essential to be able to connect with people in the pursuit of progress. If you are spending all of your time, or a great deal of it, fighting battles you will achieve little else besides warfare. The Taoist philosopher Lao Tzu once wrote, "Where armies travel, brambles grow." This Taoist thought continues to be prescient in our modern world. Are you a leader if you are combative to the point that people avoid you? Can you head an organization or team if the fierceness of your values overwhelms any opposition? How freely and honestly will people give you feedback if they realize that it is probable that any dissenting views will be squashed? The answers to these questions appear obvious but there are many people filling leadership roles who ignore them. Destroying an enemy at the cost of other's perceptions of you will not stand you in good stead for long. Conversely, making difficult decisions despite reasonable opposition and in a way that is pragmatic can help establish you as an effective person of principles. Pyrrhic victories are victories in name only. Can you really afford them?

# 7

## *"Most folks are about as happy as they make up their minds to be."*

I T IS AMAZING HOW MUCH OF OUR HAPPINESS AND SATISFACTION is dependent upon our attitude. It is possible to take a situation that certainly appears negative and transform it simply by making a positive journey of the mind. How we perceive a situation to a large extent determines its positive or negative effect. If we are given a difficult task by an uncompromising supervisor it can be easy to pull into a shell of negativity. However, taking such a journey, although seemingly natural, will result only in making the circumstances worse. If we choose to simply take a positive perspective on the happenings around us it is amazing what an impact that act has. What we think about and how we perceive things expands into our actions. If our morale is low and we dwell upon the wrongs that have been done to us then we dig a deeper hole that is ever more difficult to climb out of. On the other hand, if we take a conscious step to attempt to make the best of things and even find goodness in them then we have a greater possibility of success and wellness. Perception, to some extent, is reality. Additionally, if we surround ourselves with negative people, influences, and reminders then we may be doomed to misery. Negativity breeds itself in the spirits of all who immerse themselves in it. What we think about sets the course for our daily actions. Therefore, try to see the best in any circumstance regardless of how painful. In tragic instances this process will happen over a great deal of time but even then healing will occur if it is allowed to.

# 8

## *"No one has a good enough memory to make a successful liar."*

**I**T IS POSSIBLE TO LIE ON OCCASION AND GET BY WITH IT. However, over time, no person can be a successful leader with a reputation that does not conjure up descriptors such as honesty, integrity, and dependability. It cannot be too strongly emphasized how essential it is for a leader to be able to establish trust amongst and with those whom he or she works. Without trust no relationship can be healthy or complete. In work, as in families, the basic elements of discourse are relationships. The interactions that occur on a daily basis within an organization set a tone for that culture. If people realize that falsity is rewarded then morale will both suffer and be influenced by that reality. Insincere fawning or "brown-nosing" is a pattern of behavior that, if consistently rewarded, will warp a system. In addition, if it is common for leaders to lie about budgets, negotiations, personnel moves, or common discussion points then from the top down that organization will flounder. Credibility is grounded upon the capacity for trust that a person engenders in others. If the people you work with know that they can count on your honesty you have taken a giant step forward toward the development of a sustaining environment for growth. If, on the other hand, people cannot count on your honesty and support, then they will swiftly write you off as someone they cannot rely on. In such a situation you will become isolated and information given to you will be superficial and filtered. If that is the case your effective tenure in that position will be brief and your long-term impact negligible. Trust once lost is hard to regain. Take the precautions and energy needed to be a model of trust and, over a period of time, people will come to value you as an honest broker.

8

# 9

## *"I have always found that mercy bears richer fruits than strict justice."*

IF YOU WORK WITH PEOPLE YOU WILL HAVE OCCASION TO DEAL with their foibles. It would be a wonderful world if people never did foolish or destructive things but that is just not the case. It is the lot of supervisors and leaders to have to handle complex personnel matters. In some cases the issues are so large that little can be done save stepping aside and letting the lawyers work things out. Still, this level of complexity is not the rule and in many instances a supervisor can step in and deal with the problem one-on-one with the person in question. When dealing with a disciplinary matter the tendency may be to take the bull by the horns and make sure this never happens again. Yet, in the real world it should be realized that the person who you put in their place today will be there to face you in the future. It is wrong to avoid dealing with problems. Such a style results in a diminution of quality within a system and sets a bad example for everyone in the organization. Problems do not simply vanish but they can be handled directly or indirectly. If a person's mistake is an honest one bred from good intentions handle it from a supportive approach. Sometimes problems result from ignorance and the acceptable solution is to provide information. In other instances the result was unforeseen or because of a person making poor decisions based upon inexperience. In those situations handle the core issue and make sure the person knows what to do in the future. Sometimes the person is so chagrined by what they did that all you need to do is listen to them castigate themselves. For those rare but self-evident hard heads who see nothing wrong with their hurtful behavior, these are the people who you should use the full extent of your authority to handle. However, in most cases mistakes that occur are remediable and may well be best served by offering guidance and a form of systemic mercy. Remember that you should treat others, as you would wish to be treated. A person who bases their career on meting out merciless "justice" may end up isolated and shunned if they are not careful.

# 10

## *"Practice proves more than theory."*

**I**T IS EASY TO PONTIFICATE ON MATTERS THAT OTHERS WILL HAVE to operationalize. There are leaders who consider themselves "idea people" but have very little capacity for getting detailed work done. A philosophy, vision, or mission is an important part of any successful organization. The core beliefs that drive the way in which an organization functions are lynchpins in the provision of service to customers. But, if those elements are mere documents that hang on the wall without operational validity they are worse than worthless. Systems that have "big ideas" and no practical way of getting them to work are headed for trouble. These are systems that like to bandy about words such as restructuring, reorganization, and re-tooling while simultaneously having little understanding of how portions of the organization actually work. Leaders who adopt this form of operation alienate people. They create an atmosphere where co-workers see themselves and their work affected by changes that seem to make no sense. In such workplaces there is a fundamental gap between ideas and their implementation. Leaders who are able to mobilize the human resources in their systems to address problems in a cohesive and functional manner must bridge that gap. If the theory behind an initiative is not open to testing then such a problem solving nexus will never occur. Strong leaders are able to see their opinions dissected and even abandoned if the data says they should be. Such a situation will breed a cohesion that better prepares the key players for handling even the most complex issue. Conversely, a leader who considers themselves above the details of solving problems created by their philosophy will breed discontent and even disaster. If you are more of an "idea person" surround yourself with good lieutenants who can get the job done. Otherwise you risk the dilemma of a performance gap that comes from reaching too far for goals that are little understood.

# 11

## *"Leave nothing for tomorrow that can be done today."*

IN A HIGH STAKES WORLD IT CAN BE ALL TOO EASY TO BECOME overwhelmed by the demands of work. There always seems to be another person to talk to, report to complete, meeting to attend, or project to address. In such a situation the tendency to leave some things for the future can develop. Try to resist that temptation. If you can complete a task today get it done while the opportunity exists. Windows of opportunity open and then close. If such a window presents itself to you seize it. You never know what tomorrow will bring. Conversely, if you are beating your head against the proverbial wall to develop a solution to a given problem step back and let things sit for a while. Amazing though it may seem, some of the most intricate problems can find their solution if you let it come to you. It is possible to overwork a problem and leave yourself chasing your tail. If you pause and let ideas emerge you might stand a better chance of coming up with an effective alternative than simply banging away with a tired brain. Work that can be completed in a timely manner will allow you some reflective time down the road. Further, if you get something done you will be less stressed by the inevitable & unanticipated issues that will arise. There is virtually always a crisis or perceived crisis that needs your attention. Would it not be better to have other items checked off your "to do" list when those fires start to blaze? However, while pursuing work completion bear in mind that "workaholism" is a disease and not a virtue. Do not sacrifice your family, health, or well being in the name of work completion. No reasonable organization will want its members crushing themselves in the pursuit of the completion of tasks. That is a surefire pathway to illness or frustration.

# 12

## *"We must not promise what we ought not, lest we be called upon to perform what we cannot."*

**B**E CAREFUL WHAT YOU PROMISE BECAUSE PEOPLE WILL EXPECT you to deliver. One of the most common mistakes that leaders make is to flippantly make commitments that they really have no intention or ability to fulfill. If you say you are going to be at a meeting be sure you get there. If you tell a person that you can deliver the goods you better be able to or they will learn to doubt you. Credibility is based upon a variety of things amongst which is your dependability. Your word does go a long way toward defining your reputation. If you are a leader who people can rest assured will follow through in the way you say you will then your level of trust amongst colleagues will soar. If, on the other hand, you are inconsistent on follow through people will quickly learn that you are a "no account" who makes promises that cannot or will not be kept. In some situations the damage of an errant promise can be smashing. If, for example, you promise a colleague that you will be able to arrange their promotion and then fail to deliver, what basis do you have for maintaining a relationship with that person in the future? Or, what about promising your boss that you can deliver a completed report that will "wow" the board at the next monthly meeting and then find yourself flopping? Be sure that when you make a promise you take every step that can be taken to make things happen. Surely there will be situations when a well-intended promise is defeated by unforeseen or unexpected circumstance. In such a situation people may understand that fate was against you and it was not really your fault. However, if you make a habit of failing to deliver on your word you will be written off.

## <u>13</u>

*"I am not bound to win, but I am bound to be true. I am not bound to succeed, but I am bound to live up to what I have. I must stand by anybody that stands right and part company with him when he goes wrong."*

**T**HERE IS NOTHING EASY ABOUT BEING A LEADER. THE WEIGHT of responsibility can rest heavily upon your shoulders. There are days when you will question why you chose to follow the trail you have selected. But even the most difficult path leads to something. It is essential that you have some sense of what your core values and essential beliefs are. Those core values serve as your trail map and help guide each and every footstep that you take. If you are untrue to those beliefs you will know it. If, over time, you consistently are forced to violate those beliefs you will either corrupt yourself or search for another position. There will be times when you must decide whether or not you will stand by other people who you perceive as in the right but who, none the less, make up a minority perspective. This will be a test of both your beliefs and character. Such a test will come will little announcement and you must be prepared for it. The best preparation is to understand what your principles are. What is the essence of your work philosophy? Are these values congruent with how you live your life? Do you model the values that you purport to hold? If you do not know the answers to these questions you may struggle to cope with them when they are asked. If you do know how to answer these questions, and your answers are based upon positive principles that support growth, then you will prosper and become eminently armed to survive even the slings and arrows of professional defeat. We are defined by our inner beliefs and not by the judgments, attacks, or insults of those around us.

# 14

## *"Whenever I hear anyone arguing for slavery, I feel the strong impulse to see it tried on him personally."*

T HERE ARE PEOPLE IN POSITIONS OF AUTHORITY WHO EXPECT their employees to sacrifice whatever they may value in order to fulfill the wishes of the leader. Such unbending personalities see nothing wrong with staff members having to burn the midnight oil to complete assignments given at the last minute. It is nothing to such a boss to hand off a project to a staff member that requires weeks to accomplish but expect it done in a matter of days. Such powerbrokers often declaim about the work ethic they have and how sacrifices in the name of organizational priorities are necessary. In some instances such workhorse leaders are also willing to sacrifice their own private lives and demonstrate this "commitment" by putting in massive amounts of hours while expecting others to follow their example. In other cases, a leader may expect his or her underlings to put their nose to the grindstone while the boss goes home to enjoy the weekend. As we all know "rank doth have its privileges" but there are limits. The fallacy inherent in all of these postures is that they border upon enslavement while lacking authenticity. Yes, the work at hand must be accomplished and that is the way of the world. However, life only occurs once and if we fail to grasp the ring of opportunity to enjoy a fulfilling life what have we gained in that bargain? Is work more important than attending your children's school events? Can you rationally exchange time with your family for a completion of a few more pages of a report that may well gather dust on an office shelf? A leader who is more than willing to dispose of your family and leisure time in the name of "productivity" is no friend. Rather, what he or she is doing is slowly but surely whittling away your basic humanity in pursuit of questionable outcomes. Only you can determine what price you are willing to pay for glory. But, as you calculate that cost be sure to honestly assess what you are paying and to whom.

# 15

## *"Always bear in mind that your own resolution to succeed is more important than any other thing."*

I N ANY TASK, YOU MUST BELIEVE IN THE POSSIBILITY OF SUCCESS or it is unlikely to ensue. If you are a leader in charge of a difficult assignment you must model confidence or those working with you will live to see their morale fade. Do not hide hard truths from those you are teaming with. If the odds are against success be sure that each team member has a clear understanding of that fact and then work together to find the best possible way to overcome those long odds. Victory in the face of great odds is a distinct possibility. Who would have predicted that a poorly educated lad born in the backwoods areas of Kentucky and reared in poverty and want would have ascended to the White House and defended the interests of the Republic during the Civil War? The rise of Abraham Lincoln to that critical and terminal post was an amazing journey. Such seemingly miraculous results can occur but they require preparation, effort, and a belief in the possibility of success. It is your role as the leader to set the table for victory. In carrying out that act you serve not only yourself but also the interests of each team member and the people you serve. Begin by convincing yourself that a successful outcome can be achieved and then move on to help lead others to that desired result.

# 16

## *"Better to remain silent and be thought a fool than to speak out and remove all doubt."*

THERE ARE TIMES TO SPEAK AND TIMES TO BE QUIET. IT MAY take time and experience to discern when to jump into the fray and offer an opinion and when not to. But, being able to make this judgment is an essential survival skill for a leader. Have you ever worked with or for a person who could never refrain from talking and did so at great length? This can truly be an exhausting experience. Conversely, have you ever tried to have an important conversation with a person who was so reticent that all you came away with was an image of a human being who was doing a perfect imitation of an ER patient who was "flat-lining"? There is a delicate balance that separates strong communicators with common sense from people to be avoided in meetings. In looking at this communication issue a few key points should be borne in mind. First, be concise and stay on topic and people will appreciate you more. Be aware of time parameters and in a meeting be sure you do not tie up people's time unnecessarily via your commentary. In some situations you need to read the public and, if necessary, refrain from saying anything. Remember that timing is everything. Do not interrupt people unless they are monopolizing the conversation. Then, make them pause, restate a few of their points in a reflective way, and move the meeting along. If someone else has already made your point do not feel compelled to make it again—such behavior will not be appreciated and drags things out. Silence is OK and there are times when you are better served simply listening. When others are speaking truly listen and exhibit non-verbal behaviors that confirm that you are attending. Try to remember the Taoist saying, "Am I listening, or merely waiting to speak." If you must air a controversial viewpoint do so but acknowledge

18

that this may be a minority view but that it should be heard. If a consensus has been determined and you disagree, state your opinions and then loyally carry out the team's decision. If, over time, you find yourself consistently in the minority and carrying out dictates you cannot support then think about your place in the organization and, if necessary, consider other options.

# 17

## *"Time is everything."*

IF YOU FAIL TO REALIZE WHAT AN IMPORTANT RESOURCE TIME IS then you have missed the boat. There is no more important gift that you can give to any person or group of people than your time. If you have worked effectively in a system for a number of years you have made the greatest contribution through your gift of time. The time you set aside to commune with your family or friends is golden. Likewise, time given up to work related efforts also is as a major contribution to the people your organization serves. Every decision you make involves time as a resource. Will you attend this meeting or work on a proposal? Do you have enough time to accept the offer to sit on a committee? Can you do an adequate job on the two projects you have to plan for or should you ask for help with one of them? Everything involves the juggling of competing priorities and a concomitant effect upon your time. Thus, you need to be effective in how you manage time or you will end up endlessly struggling to stay on top of things. In such a situation something will suffer. You might end up sacrificing family and recreational time due to faulty planning. Conversely, you might not be able to adequately prioritize task sequencing and thereby falter at work. Time can work for or against you within your mind. In reality there is only so much time and that is a constant figure moving at a seamlessly given rate. However, our perception of time varies depending upon our mindset. Some afternoons or nights seem endless and delicious. On other days, we seem to be fighting a losing battle against a shrinking clock. Leaders must harness time and make it a realistic ally. They must also fully realize what their core priorities are and dedicate the majority of their precious time to them.

# 18

## *"When you've got an elephant by the hind leg, and he is trying to run away, it's best to let him run."*

E FFECTIVE LEADERS KNOW WHEN TO CUT THEIR LOSSES AND LET go. While it is important to advocate for your positions there are times when it is simply not going to go your way.

When you realize that it is indeed time to throw in the towel—do so. It is not only bad judgment but also self-defeating to push forward when tactical and strategic sense dictates against it. In the military there is the very essential concept of a strategic withdrawal. Rather than expend ever more resources on a lost cause prudent judgment dictates detachment from an advance. Such acknowledgements are far more sensible than ignoring reality in the face of overwhelming odds. For example, if it is obvious that a certain negotiation ploy is simply not going to fly and, worse yet, will derail the entire proceeding, step back and recognize the limitations of the situation. Such a strategy will move you into a more approachable circumstance and will cement your reputation for reasonableness. Conversely, to hold tight to an unwinable approach will result in acrimony, discord, and a reputation of intransigence. Leaders who persist when every one around them is counseling compromise are often dictatorial in their nature. It can be very difficult for this type of personality to coalesce with the idea that they cannot have their way. This is an understandable but relatively immature posture to take and will not assist anyone to solve problems. To be an effective problem solver you have to know when to give up. Once you have made that choice let go of the emotional energy that goes along with the task. There may be a tendency to dwell on the events as a failure or in a "what if" mode. Do not succumb to these temptations as they are a waste of energy and will lead to maudlin mulling. Move on to the next challenge and reflect in a productive way on your experiences.

# 19

## *"A house divided against itself cannot stand."*

A TEAM IS NOT A TEAM UNLESS ITS MEMBERS ARE UNITED IN THE pursuit of common goals. If a leader cannot harness the minds and spirits of team members in such an endeavor then productivity will dip. Individuals can be amazingly effective due to their innate talents. However, synergy that results from collectives pooling their individual resources can far surpass the outputs of individual members. One of the most significant charges for a leader is to develop strategies that create the bonds of common loyalty, understanding, and mission and which, in turn, drive people forward because of their innate desire to serve. Most people have a sincere wish to be productive. It is a minority of people who long to go to work and function in a non-productive fashion. Yet, the majority of people surveyed nationally typically express dissatisfaction with their work. One of the primary reasons for this type of global job dissatisfaction is the way in which institutions treat people. In far too many instances supervisors work in a high-handed and dehumanizing way. Such ill treatment leads to disgruntlement and frustration. When people begin to adopt a negative mindset they fragment rather than group together as positive team members. Unhealthy cultures breed disenfranchisement and factionalism. An organization wherein people simply want to be left alone to do their work or just "get by" is not one that will optimize customer service. As Lincoln noted, a social network that is splintered over major issues will entropy. Leaders must make the maintenance of common goals and high morale a centerpiece of their efforts. Unless unity is established in a healthy way within a group how can the seeds of teamwork be sown?

# 20

*"Let us have faith that right makes might; and in that faith, to the end, dare to do our duty, as we understand it."*

IF YOU WISH TO BE A LEADER YOU WILL NEED TO BE ABLE TO make decisions and face the consequences of them. Every day you will be tested in terms of the choices you are called upon to make. Should I say yes to this staff member's request for a professional leave? Will we move this person to a new assignment? How am I going to deal with this unhappy customer? Every issue that you face will require decisions on your part and people will be watching and recalling what you do. But, the fact that you are in a position of leadership does not mean that you are acting in a solitary manner at all times. Many decisions can flow out of group processes. Indeed, some of the more long-lasting decisions are those that have grassroots support. If the ownership of a decision, even if it results in a failure, is broad-based then there is a greater likelihood of acceptance than one that is made in a "top-down" fashion. By their very nature, most people resent highhanded decisions made by leaders who come across as dictators. There can be an arrogance of power that virtually says to workers, "I am the boss and I can make whatever decision I want to!" This type of controlling leadership can exercise power through fear and force of will but it will alienate so many people that, once the dictator has left the scene, much of what he or she built crumbles back down into the dust of history. Yet, there are times when tough decisions have to be made to the displeasure of many. Leaders must be able to face the arithmetic of decision-making. The cost of easing away from necessary but difficult decisions will, in the long run, be far steeper that implementing them. If you are making an unpopular decision but you strongly sense the need to do so you must explain your reasons and check for success after implementation. If you were wrong acknowledge it and retrench. If you were right work to develop ambassadors of acceptance who will demonstrate the appropriateness of the decision through their efforts and advocacy. Hopefully, over time, people will see the rightness of the course and even adopt it as their own idea.

# <u>21</u>

*"Nothing valuable can be lost by taking time. If there be an object to hurry any of you, in hot haste, to a step which you would never take deliberately, that object will be frustrated by taking time; but no good object can be frustrated by it."*

W E LIVE IN A HURLY-BURLY WORLD. EVERYTHING APPEARS TO be split second in terms of time frame. We rush across our days with calendars that are filled to overflowing. Even children's schedules are jam packed with schoolwork, clubs, recitals, and a host of other extra-curricular efforts. In such a world it behooves us to take some time to catch our breath and think. Nowhere is this more relevant than in the case of leadership. Many people will come to a leader with issues that are germane to them. In fact, many people present their needs to a leader as if they were a pressing and immediate crisis. Given the number of requests for help that are apt to come a leader's way in a given day it is a vital survival skill to be able to have a decision making style that allows you to clarify what is a real and what is a perceived crisis. Every decision does not need to be made on the spot. While there are legitimate crisis that require immediate attention these are the minority of instances. If you can develop a habit of taking some time to sort out a situation before you leap into making a decision you will probably make more sound decisions than if you rush to judgement. Giving yourself some time to reflect upon the data affords you greater clarity of thought and better application of your analytical resources to the problems at hand. By telling people that you will get back to them in a day or so after you have had a chance to think about their needs and then coming up with a reasonable option you will, over a period of time, cement your reputation as a thoughtful leader. Snap decisions can be very good but, if that is your standard mode of decision-making, you will become prone to short sightedness in your operation. Also, a leader who handles everything on the spot fuels an environment where everything becomes a crisis. In such a setting all problems can become bigger than life. You cannot allow perspective to be lost or you will constantly be putting out fires rather than leading.

# 22

## *"Every blade of grass is a study."*

THE WORLD AROUND US IS INCREDIBLY COMPLEX AND interconnected. We sometimes make the mistake of failing to realize how woven into the web of life each and every one of us is. Human beings all too often demonstrate an arrogance of action in the way they handle the environment and other life forms. In some beliefs mankind is seen as "the crown of creation" rather than simply one of a multitude of life forms that cohabitate and affect one another across the globe. In reality, it can be argued that all life is amazing in its complexity and grandeur. How can we evaluate the importance of one life form versus another? Likewise, what parts of the environment around the world are more or less important than another? As Lincoln noted in this brief but reflective statement everything around us, down to a single blade of grass, has complexity that is amazing to behold. This trait of value exists in all the people we encounter in our daily lives. Every individual who you supervise has a history, hopes, dreams, fears, and uniqueness. Their idiosyncrasies are part of the patchwork quilt of life that makes up not only the organization they work in but also the broader world around us. If we touch their lives we leave an emotional footprint that changes both them and ourselves. Like ripples in a pond when a pebble is thrown into it, our interaction with another person radiates out through many unseen faces that are indirectly affected by that relationship. Thus, a leader should be aware of the impact that his or her behavior has on those people who work with them. A simple act of compassion can have untold benefit not only for the giver and receiver but also for many other people who will inherit the karma of that action. If we stop and think about the fact that all life has value we will be better prepared to treat it with respect. A kind word, a gentle gesture, the act of listening, or a pat on the back can have meaning that we do not even understand. Take the time to study those around you and learn to value them as living beings with hearts and spirits to nurture and be nurtured by. Then, you will be surprised by the results that might be attained.

# 23

## *"Half finished work generally proves to be labor lost."*

T HERE ARE PEOPLE WHO START A SERIES OF PROJECTS, WORK very hard on them, get part way through, and then move on to something else leaving a sequence of partially completed jobs trailing behind them like a string of sentence fragments running across the pages of a semi-completed novel. In many cases such individuals are bright and capable people brimming with ideas. In the right context such creative force individuals can be a vital part of a team. But, if such a person is placed in a leadership role the danger of institutional disorientation is quite real. One guiding principal for leaders is that while multi-tasking is a necessary survival skill, it is improbable that any single person, or related group of team members, will be able to orchestrate massive changes unless they are able to focus concentrated time & energy to bring component parts of the broader projects to fruition before delving into other domains of change. Simply put—finish what you start and then move on. Yes, in a complex organization there will be a constant need to address a variety of issues within the same decision making box or time frame. Yet, by being overly ambitious a leader runs the very real risk of fragmenting the attention of organizational personnel to such an extent that the mere arithmetic laws of probability will determine that some, or all, of the initiatives will have major problems at the same time. Pace yourself and try to work within the confines of reasonableness when working on projects. There may certainly be occasions when stress due to multi-tasking is great but, if you use a sound & pragmatic approach to what you place on your plate and the plates of your colleagues, you stand a better chance of producing both completed and successful work.

## 24

*"I know nothing so pleasant to the mind, as the discovery of anything that is at once new and valuable."*

LEADERS MUST BE LEARNERS. IF YOU WISH TO LEAD PEOPLE YOU need to have a deeply felt commitment to enhancing what you know. While such a pursuit of knowledge should encompass work-related skills it is best if the focus of learning is even broader. For example, an educational administrator serving as a principal should peruse professional journals, learn about instructional methodologies, study books dealing with child development, and attend appropriate workshops. These sorts of professional development activities are necessary so that the principal in question remains in touch with best practices in her or his field and thereby can better serve the children, parents, and colleagues within the school. However, the principal in question should also study, read, and pursue other forms of learning so that he or she has a broadened understanding of intellectual curiosity. By reading children's books, studying about science, traveling, or watching movies a leader can have more to offer to everyone around them. It is a boring situation indeed when all a person has to talk about is work. Is it not better to be able to discuss books, recount recently viewed films, describe art, or share vacation stories? Building a team and being a dynamic leader requires a level of acumen that functions on a daily basis. By studying and learning a leader is in a position to both sharpen their wits and offer more to those around them. Life-long learning is a noble pursuit and one that will stand you in good stead when you attempt to develop meaningful professional relationships with your colleagues and other people you serve.

# 25

*"If we could first know where we are, and whither we are tending, we could then better judge what to do, and how to do it."*

CHANGE FOR CHANGE SAKE ALONE IS USUALLY A POOR handmaiden of an idea. There are leaders who make a career out of joining organizations for the sole purpose of topsy-turvy change. Such individuals generally stay around in an organization long enough to cause chaos and then disappear leaving a ruined city of a system behind them. In order to leverage change you need to know the historical variables inherent in an organization, understand the current state of operations, and have a clear vision of where the system should be heading. This type of change process will still engender discomfort in some group members as people generally are at least somewhat anxious about changes. However, by having a cognitive map that is somewhat clearly marked a leader stands a far better chance of staging a successful change process than by blindly striking out into the woods. Before embarking on a change initiative take the time to adequately plan what the process will probably look like. Bear in mind that unforeseen variables will arise and flexibility must be built into the plan. Still, if you have taken adequate time and involved the right stakeholders in the planning process you stand a much better chance of staging this change initiative in a productive way. The alternative is to do what many organizations do and that is to muddle through ill thought out change only to find yourself back where you started months or years later. Such a thoughtless approach will result in lowered productivity, employee distrust, and an institutional memory bank that will be more cynical & resistant to future change suggestions regardless of how thoughtful they may be.

## 26

*"The world will little note, nor long remember what we say here, but it can never forget what they did here."*

PRIDE GOETH BEFORE THE FALL. IT IS EASY TO DEVELOP AN EGO as a leader but it is difficult to function effectively if you do. Leadership is as much a product of personality as any other factor. We lead in a way that reflects who we are. If we are egotists then we will swagger our way through our leadership careers leaving a footprint behind that, while memorable, will probably not be appreciated by those people whose lives we touched. On the other hand, if we realize that humility is an essential virtue, we may well be better prepared to handle the demands incumbent in being a leader. It is important to realize that, regardless of how much responsibility we have, nothing we do will endure forever. Every decision we make is transitory in its elemental nature. While some choices carry much higher stakes than others do, very few decisions are going to fundamentally alter reality. By realizing the limitations to our power, control, and influence we place our work, as leaders, into a more realistic perspective. Further, it is also essential to realize that the people we lead, who do the actual productive work in the front lines, are at the core of an organization's success. Leaders who become too full of their own greatness will detach themselves from both reality and those whom they lead. Successes in an organization are the result of many people's efforts. Leaders who take credit for the good times in a system will lose the faith of their team members. A leader without followers is no leader at all. In order to be a vibrant and visionary leader you must check your pride at the door and then go forward in a confidant and sharing mode. Then ask yourself this fundamental question, "Am I leading this group for my own empowerment or to serve?"

# 27

*"I shall never be old enough to speak without embarrassment when I have nothing to talk about."*

EVERYONE MAKES MISTAKES AND SOME OF THEM ARE memorable. If you have done something that is embarrassing the best strategy is to take your disquietude as the price of your actions and move on. It is hard to face failure or ridicule. No one in their right mind would set out to act in a way that shows them in a poor light. Yet, regardless of how competent a leader may be there will be inevitable circumstances that show off their weaknesses or chinks in their armor. If you have made a mistake that leads others to have ammunition for criticizing you there is no way to deny reality. Admit your error and move ahead. If you dwell on a negative circumstance you accomplish nothing constructive. In fact, by fixating on your foibles and reliving them you allow yourself to be stuck in the rut of failure. It makes little sense to prolong your anguish by replaying the embarrassing moment over and over in your mind. In carrying out that repetitive mental refrain you act in a way that is far more onerous than even your sharpest critic. There are enough people out there in the world waiting to be critical of others without adding your own internal fuel to that firestorm of attack. Instead, admit what has happened, make whatever acknowledgements that need to occur, reflect on what you can learn from the situation, and let it go. There is great power in forgiveness. Therefore, allow yourself to forgive the actions in question, and become your own friend rather than your sharpest critic.

# 28

## *"When the conduct of men is designed to be influenced, persuasion, kind, unassuming persuasion, should ever be adopted."*

S OLVING PROBLEMS THAT ARISE AMONG PEOPLE REQUIRES THE ability to negotiate and persuade others that a solution is first possible and then desirable. People are amazing creatures. They are capable of great good and seemingly unfathomable cruelty. Many, times when a problem arises among individuals it can appear insoluble. Mediating interpersonal difficulties requires a steady emotional hand and a clear mind. Still, when an opportunity arises to help mediate such a conflict a peacemaker can be a veritable godsend. In order to fill the role of honest broker you will need to first convince all parties that you are open to new solutions. Unless you can convince the aggrieved players that you are willing to listen to them and then serve as a compromiser without selfish interest you will not be trusted. It is essential that you win the trust of the participants in the mediation or you will be unsuccessful. A keynote way to accomplish this task of trust building is to use careful listening skills inclusive of reflective restatements. By carefully taking in what has been said and then summarizing in concise and sincere restatements a facilitator can set the stage for compromise. Further, such honest approaches allow all players to have a real sense that they are being heard and understood. In such instances the probability of rational processing increases while the likelihood of emotional clashes lessens. Finally, once the option for compromise comes about a skilled mediator will help bridge the final gap of resolution by summarizing and offering potential compromises. In the end, perhaps the best leadership gift that a person can have is the ability to bring conflict-laden groups together and mend fences. If you can do this complex task others will look to you for support in tough times and thus respect you.

# 29

## *"I am here; I must do the best I can, and bear the responsibility of taking the course which I feel I ought to take."*

HARRY S. TRUMAN ONCE SAID, "IF YOU CAN'T STAND THE HEAT, stay out of the kitchen." Leaders must face the music when things get rough. It is easy to be a ship captain when the seas are as smooth as glass. But, when a storm blows across Lake Superior, the captain and crew have to earn their wages. Leaders need to work in such a way that conflict is lessened or prevented even before it occurs through careful preparation. Yet, regardless of how skilled a leader is there will inevitably be difficult problems that have to be addressed. In these situations the leader must suck up their courage and muster the fortitude necessary to face the charge. Being a leader in a conflictual situation is not what most people want to have a steady diet of. Yet, conflict is a necessary part of life. Without struggle progress is rarely possible. One need only think about the way in which each of us entered the world to realize that the birth of anything of value will require effort, sweat, and struggle. It is how well you perform in these pressurized situations that will fundamentally determine how you are perceived as a leader. If you can weather the storms that sometimes arise in your field then others will look to you as a force of accomplishment and a person who can be counted on even in the most difficult circumstances. Conversely, if you lurk in the shadows, push minions forward into the fray while you lollygag in the background, or fail to take the measure of the situation, your reputation will sag. You earn your salary as a leader by working through the hard struggles and thereby buying time and resource capital to make progress in positive directions. If you can handle the worst that your position offers you will be resilient enough to produce the best.

# 30

## *"I determined to be so clear that no honest man could misunderstand me and no dishonest one could successfully misrepresent me."*

IN COMMUNICATION PERHAPS NO QUALITY IS MORE IMPORTANT than clarity. It is of little value to be a dynamic speaker who projects nothing of substance. Have you ever listened to a political candidate or supervisor who spoke in a ministerial way but, after you were finished listening to them, you were unable to recall anything of specific value that they said? If you mean to say something be sure that your words match your intent. There is little point in addressing people and then communicating nothing of importance. Likewise, if you are writing a memo, report, or brief make sure that the words you impart to the page cover the subject at hand in a way that is purposeful. Pretty words and flowery expressions may sound good but they will ring falsely if they have no depth. A leader who consistently speaks without saying anything will swiftly lose the attention of his or her team. People want to have a leader who can put their thoughts into words. If you can capture the moment in essential language others will look to you as someone who actually has something worthwhile to say. Your message as a leader is an expression of the core values that you possess. While you should not function as a preacher you are a steward of certain ideas and beliefs. If you can help others to understand the central message through your communication gifts then the probability of forward motion is increased. If you choose, instead, to engage in meaningless platitudes, arcane expressions, or false praise you will lose both the focus and confidence of those who work with you.

# 31

## *"Bad promises are better broken than kept."*

T HERE ARE TIMES WHEN A PLEDGE OR DECISION YOU HAVE MADE proves a mistake. In those cases an effective leader realizes the error of his or her ways and cuts their losses. If you persist in maintaining a position when all evidence has shown you that it was a mistake, then every moment that you pursue your faulty pathway is akin to getting more and more willfully lost. It takes some strength of character to admit when a promise was a mistake. There is a natural tendency to want to deny reality and hope that things will simply get better on their own. This tendency may be quite natural but it is based upon fantasy and not reality. In fact psychologists call such a self-defeating process an "escalation of commitment." In such a circumstance an individual, or group, pours more & more resources into a losing cause. Reasonable feedback advising a retreat or alternative strategy is rejected and may even spur on an even more vigorous playing of a losing hand. In the end this type of an "escalation of commitment" worsens results and can disable a system. As a leader you are bound to place the common good of the organization, its members, and those you serve above your own vanity. If you must retrench and change directions so be it. If you realize that a person you hired is not remediable or suited to their post then the onus rests upon you to make the necessary changes. Every time you resist the need to rethink a past decision you stultify the possibility of growth in your system. You are pledged to carry out the humane yet required hard tasks that fall on your agenda. Shrinking away from these tasks will mark you as both inefficient and directionless. When the time comes to weigh ongoing loyalty to a position once deemed good and the need to change courses you must place the greater good ahead of your own hesitation. Recognizing bad investments and getting out of them is a survival skill in the world of business as well as in the field of leadership.

# 32

*"Don't shoot too high—aim lower and the common people will understand you. They are the ones you want to reach—at least they are the ones you ought to reach. The educated and refined people will understand you anyway. If you aim too high your ideas will go over the head of the masses, and only hit those who need no hitting."*

Y OUR CHOICE OF WORDS IS AN IMPORTANT ONE. IF YOU mismatch the type of vocabulary, delivery style, or content with your audience you might as well be speaking a foreign language. Likewise, the manner in which you present information should be such that you connect with the people involved. For example, if you are meeting with parents who are hard working people with limited education you need to be aware that the use of polysyllabic words may create a barrier. Be direct and to the point & do not talk down to people. Do not assume that a person without a college degree is not highly intelligent. Further, if you use your choice of words as either a weapon geared toward intimidation or as a camouflage of your real intent—you will fail. People see through phoniness. Their realization may not always be instantaneous but the patina of smoothness that covers a more base content will wear off. Once folks realize that what you said sounded substantive but really meant nothing, they will bitterly resent you. Use straightforward language and refrain from using professional jargon that may be confusing. If you are in a position to facilitate a meeting with people who appear confused or ill at ease be sure to ask them if they have questions. Further, if a team member is using overly complex language do not hesitate to ask them to explain what they are saying. It is a good strategy to ask questions you think the customers may wish to insert but are hesitant to do so. For example, there is no shame in saying, "I probably am the only person in the group who is a little unclear about what you mean when you talk about phonemic awareness in reading—what does that really mean?" By being secure enough to take on the burden of asking clarification questions you both ease the tensions involved in uncertainty while also allowing for greater understanding on the part of the constituents in a meeting. The bottom line is that the communication tone used in a transaction must be one that is mutually understandable and fair or it will only create barriers.

## 33

*"I have never had a policy; I have simply tried to do what seemed best each day as each day came."*

WHILE IT IS IMPORTANT FOR A LEADER TO HAVE CLEARLY understood core values he or she must also be a pragmatist. The concept of situational leadership is one that serves leaders well. The ability to be flexible and react in varied ways to changing circumstances is a trait that marks effective leaders. On the one hand a leader must have a central bank of beliefs that guide the overarching way in which he or she operates. If you do not have a moral compass you will drift across the seas of life in a meandering and unfulfilling manner. Likewise, if you are a dogmatic thinker who sees only one way to handle most situations you will run afoul of the reality that the world is eminently complex and changeable. There are many people who bank on a philosophy that allows them to feel certain about what is right or wrong. Fundamentalist thinkers are very sure of what actions are permissible or not both in their lives and in those of all the people who surround them. In reality, there are very few perpetual truths that can be banked on. A leader must be able to assess situations and draw from their personal resources to find a variety of possible decision-making approaches. Trying to force every problem situation into a singular or limited subset of possibilities is a surefire way to fail. Take each situation as it comes to you and try to look at it in a flexible yet decisive way. This approach does not mean that you should junk your beliefs and values. Rather, this tact infers that while using your moral foundation you attempt to find differing and creative ways to solve problems as they come along. On a day-by-day basis life passes you by. If you try to fit all of it into one box you will find that a difficult and frustrating task. Conversely, avoiding dogma and taking things as they are, may well be a more successful approach to living and leading.

# 34

### *"I don't like to hear cut-and-dried sermons. No—when I hear a man preach, I like to see him act as if he were fighting bees."*

I T IS GOOD TO SHOW ENTHUSIASM. INDEED, PASSION IS A QUALITY that often marks some of the finest leaders. Who would wish to follow a passionless robot that shows little external emotion or love of their work? It is not only acceptable but recommended that a leader engage in a passionate pursuit of excellence. Also, it is very sound thinking to believe that by showing sincere concern for the people you work with you will help establish a compassionate and productive culture in your organization. Showing passion does not mean that you must necessarily be as animated as Mr. Lincoln suggests in this quote. Your own personality will determine the degree and manner in which your passion is demonstrated. However, if you wish to connect with the people you serve you will need to demonstrate that you have an emotional commitment to both them and the work at hand. Strong teams bond together over not only the work they do but also, and perhaps more fully, because of the relationships that are developed. In a very real sense almost all of the work that human beings do in complex organizations is grounded upon relationships. It will be difficult for a leader to be successful unless he or she realizes that human relationships are the bedrock of the work that they supervise and engage in. At the heart of relationships are emotional connections of like, dislike, hatred, compassion, and a host of other feelings. To ignore the emotional world of relationships is to potentially doom a leader to a career based upon narrowness, isolation, and ignorance. Leaders who discount this relational element in human organizations are missing the forest for the trees. Good things simply will not happen unless people feel a sense of pride and purpose grounded upon commitment to what they do and whom they do it with.

# 35

## *"Laughter is the joyous, beautiful, universal evergreen of life."*

L IFE IS FAR TOO SHORT TO BE TAKEN SERIOUSLY ALL THE TIME. Humor is a great elixir that can sustain and heal. Using humor to break the ice in some situations can be one of the smartest acts that a leader can engage in. Tension can be broken through a simple joke or a bit of irreverence. Of course, the use of humor at the wrong time or in bad taste is a foolish act. Yet, in the right way and to good purpose, humor is a wonderful release. A leader who can laugh out loud will stand a far better chance of succeeding than one who is dour. People do not gravitate toward humorless individuals. Working for someone with no apparent sense of humor can be disconcerting, boring, and disheartening. Everything in the workplace is not based upon funereal tones. If people cannot laugh they may be more prone to cry. The atmosphere in an organization is a huge contributor to factors such as job satisfaction, employee longevity, and morale. Teams that can laugh together and not take everything all too seriously are better prepared to unite in time of crisis. Life requires perspective. If you are a person who is always moaning about how overworked you are or how bad things have become, the people around you will grow tired of your demeanor. Wet blankets do not provide warmth in a rainstorm and are to be avoided. Who needs a black hole of negativity that descends into their lives whenever you arrive? Try to find the silver lining in each and every day and your work will begin to seem better than it was before. To tell a joke, kid around, or simply not take everything too seriously may be one strategy that will assist you, and those co-workers around you, to feel better about what you do. A leader who encourages a good-humored environment does a great service to all concerned. If we can laugh together we can work together. If not, then is work going to be very fulfilling?

# 36

## *"The better part of one's life consists of friendships."*

HAVE YOU EVER STOPPED TO THINK ABOUT THE PEOPLE WHO you consider friends? Friendship is so essential to people that those who are deprived of it generally feel lost. Your friends are people who care about you, share experiences, trust you, and are folks who you can count on. Without friends there would be a lessening of life's value as well as an emotional void. Leaders can become isolated. It is difficult to maintain the necessary distance that sometimes is purported to be needed between leaders and led. Work can be made so comprehensive in its nature that time ceases to exist for the vital relationships known as friendships. Do not fall into this trap. Colleagues can become close to you. While you may or may not be bosom friends you can establish meaningful and fulfilling relationships with the people you supervise. An emotionally healthy person who shares time with a group of people will become attached to members of the group simply because human beings are social creatures. Likewise, a leader who works so intensely and to the exclusion of having time for friends is one who is on the road to despair. Work is important but not more so than those activities that give us our humanity. Although the chart that a leader stares at on a daily basis can be full of emotional reefs and shoals that is no excuse for burning the midnight oil to such a degree that relationships wane. Get to know the people you work with and value them to the degree that you can. Treat those people equitably but, as you are human, recognize your differentiated relationships with each and every one of them. If you are genuine and authentic in how you open yourself up to the folks in the organization you will deepen the value of your work through the relationships that develop. If you keep your emotions bound up in a box wrapped with icy dignity you will stand alone and weep for it.

## 37

*"Forget that you have anyone to fall back upon, and you will do justice to yourself and your client."*

ALTHOUGH IT IS IMPORTANT FOR A LEADER TO KNOW WHAT resources there are available to help in different matters there must be a central core of independence that allows divergent issues to be handled independently. No system can afford a leader who must trot off to get guidance every time a tough question comes up. Of course no one knows everything or even much about most things. Still, if a person in a leadership position is unable to empower others through their own expertise why are they in that post? If you are a less experienced supervisor there is no shame in turning to resource people or materials in order to back up your concerns. Nobody enters a new field having all the answers. If they think they do they will come to realize that pride goes before the fall. There is a learning curve for new actions and it can sometimes be quite steep. However, if that curve is not traversed in a reasonable time period people will question what your capacities are. Time does not idly wait for folks to catch up to the necessities of survival. The realities of the marketplace dictate that a leader become able to get up to speed in their position in a reasonable time frame. Yet, even relatively new leaders can spread their wings and make decisions in a timely manner. If you are confronting a relatively novel problem stop and reflect on what the core of the issue is. Are you coping with an unforeseen employee crisis? Is there a financial issue that has come up that was unanticipated? Has someone in the organization done something foolish? Whatever the issue, after thinking about its parameters try to work out a reasonable solution. If you are unsure about your proposed course of action check with reliable sources for feedback. Share your initial plan of attack with those veterans and remain open to the power of suggestion. Then implement your course of action or one that is somewhat revised due to feedback received. In this way you begin to develop or refine your decision-making schema while also taking advantage of resource people who surround you. You will develop your own style of decision-making based upon independent action but that can take some time. Use the resources that exist to help shape the talents that rest within your spirit but realize that you must become independent as a leader or you will not be one.

## 38

*"I have an irresistible desire to live till I can be assured that the world is a little better for my having lived in it."*

THE CONCEPT OF SERVICE SHOULD REST AT THE CENTER OF ANY organization's mission. We walk the earth to enjoy our independent lives. That is an elemental component of every living creature's drive to survive. However, beyond our own egoistic needs there rests a more communal purpose for life. As social beings humans by and large have a sense that there is a shared duty in life. Through the act of service, good works, or compassionate practices people reach out to help other beings. This act of service to others can become the centerpiece of a person's life. Within their families they will tirelessly give of themselves to assist in the growth and nurturance of their children, spouse, parents, or other family members. Generally, such nurturing spirits will also extend that mindset out into the circle of their friends and colleagues. Through such sacrifice great personal growth can occur. Those who give to others offer a gift that rewards in two ways. First, the gift of help brings sustenance to the receiver in the obvious way. A person who needs advice, assistance, or material goods will clearly gain from their provision. Likewise, a person who receives honestly given gifts may well realize that there is humanity in a world that sometimes appears cruel. This portion of the gift is uplifting and can spread outward as the receiver in turn is the giver to other people in need. Secondly, the giver is rewarded through the inner sense that what they are doing in their life has value. Through the act of giving we reward ourselves by simply being a compassionate human being. Acts of compassion or goodness rebound back to the giver as much as they reward the receiver. In helping others we help ourselves. In a leadership position you are

47

placed in a spot where your capacity to serve others is magnified. What an opportunity you have to help someone on a daily basis. Are you seizing that ring of opportunity or is it slipping away from you? Set out now to be of assistance in some way large or small to at least one person every day and watch what you have begun.

# 39

*"Persuade your neighbors to compromise whenever you can. Point out to them how the nominal winner is often a real loser—in fees, expenses, and waste of time."*

SOME FOLKS LIKE TO ARGUE FOR ARGUMENT SAKE. THESE people seem to simply like a good scrap. They are ready, willing, and able to drop the gloves like a hockey player unexpectedly checked and go at it hammer and tongs. They may even be broadly successful in winning these engagements and seemingly getting what they want. In reality, such personages are really bullies whose influence extends only as far as fear can push it. Sadly, warfare has marred human history since the dawn of the ages. Militaristic incursions persist and boil over on a daily basis. As you read this sentence somewhere in the world some act of violence is occurring. Take solace in the fact that you are not presently involved in it. However, violence or anger will touch your life in some way in the future. That contact can simply be your presence in a work situation where a dictatorial and aggressive leader dominates a colleague. When that happens you have to make choices. If you are the observer of this circumstance you can intervene in whatever way seems reasonable to stop the aggression. If it is your boss who is the attacker you can either comfort the victim later or make whatever commentary is appropriate at the time. Over time, if you face such workplace dominance too often you must weigh out how long you can endure laboring in a system that allows such "leadership" behavior to occur. If you are the recipient of the wrath, bear in mind that what another person thinks of you and your efforts does not define them. You control the key that unlocks how you view yourself. A supervisor who rants at you or abuses you emotionally can only unlock that area of your spirit if you allow them to. Stand up for yourself in the strongest way you can. Use your inner strength to carry you through the sad situation. As the boss is talking listen but also filter his or her input through your own sense of who you are. Think whatever negative thoughts the situation merits but do not express them as they will only make things worse. Do not endure abuse but buffer the criticism of others with the medicinal value of your spirit. There may be times when you work for a pit bull. Learn what you can from that circumstance and realize that the problem rests in the boss and not in you. If times get too unbearable seek out other options or solace from those who care for you. Remember that a supervisor who treats you with cruelty teaches a lesson as to how not to handle others. Learn that lesson and refrain from passing on cruelty yourself. Remember how you felt when you were mistreated and do not treat others in that way. Negative leaders teach negative lessons which can help you to make the world better through your own travail.

## 40

*"The sharpness of a refusal or the edge of a rebuke may be blunted by an appropriate story, so as to save the wounding feeling and yet serve the purpose."*

I F YOU WORK IN A LEADERSHIP CAPACITY YOU WILL HAVE THE opportunity to give people bad news. No leader can say yes to everyone. There will be times when you will have to discipline, advise, reject, or fire other people. These situations can be very difficult and painful. No decent person wants to tell another human being that they cannot keep their job. These are high stakes conversations and they can be rather emotional. However, if you are delivering a rebuff to a co-worker you need not do so in a mean spirited manner. Even the worst news from a supervisor can be delivered in an evenhanded fashion. The way you tell someone something may well be as important as what you are telling them. If you are compassionate and clear in your message you stand a much better chance of having it heard than if you are vindictive about things. For example, if you are disciplining or correcting a veteran colleague whom you value would you do so in a manner that permanently damaged that relationship? The answer to this question is patently obvious. In such a situation you could well privately meet with the person and ask them what they think went wrong. In many instances that person will be harder on themselves than even you would think of being. If so, listen and offer feedback that is pertinent to the task of correcting the situation. If you are fair and objective in such a circumstance you can improve the rapport you have with that person through being fair and compassionate in your criticism. In other situations you will be dealing with people who probably have no business working in the field they are presently in. If so, your task as a leader is to make the tough decisions about who will work with you. If you shirk this responsibility you and the organization will suffer. You do no one a favor when you overlook a weak person and let them stay around because you do not have the stomach to do the right thing. However, even if the employee is negative, carping, and loathsome you must model professional and concerned actions. How you treat others will shape your broader performance as a leader. If you have to deliver bad news do so in a fair and decent way. Avoiding such duties or pulling out your hatchet will do nothing but label you as the poorest sort of leader.

# 41

## *"I'll study and get ready, and then the chance will come."*

I F YOUR GOAL IS TO IMPROVE YOUR CAPACITY TO DO YOUR present job or move up in an organization you must prepare yourself to do so. People will notice your work if it is noticeable. One way to make yourself and your skills obvious is to hone them. Whatever job you have you can seek out greater skills. At the very minimum you can engage in professional development geared toward at least maintaining the talents that you possess. How stifling it must be to work in a job which you think so little of that you would not even consider learning more about it. In fact, a person who holds a job in an organization who does not have a commitment to continuous growth and development is not an individual who probably is doing very much to enhance the lot of customers, co-workers, the organization, or themselves. As Stephen Covey says we must "sharpen the saw" before we take it out of the tool shed for use. A failure to hone the teeth of a saw will result in badly cut wood. Dull saws bind up in the wood and cause frustration. Such a saw can also jump out of its cut mark and hurt someone. Thus, a careful worker will attend to the saw before it is put into use. Likewise, we too must sharpen our mental and physical saws or they will react in a similar fashion. Through learning we can revitalize who we are and what we do. In a similar vein, a person who neglects their physical and mental wellness will be a dull blade. If you want to perform well in life you must prepare for it. In your work you need to seek out professional development while also thinking about your lifestyle. If you have any dreams of promotion you must look around you and within yourself to see what is going on. It is unlikely that a person who is drifting will be moved into a leadership role unless the organization itself is adrift. Take some time to learn the lessons that the system you are working in can teach you. Through such preparation you pave the highway of capability that may well lead you to your next professional destination.

# 42

## *"I am a patient man—always willing to forgive on the Christian terms of repentance, and also to give ample time for repentance."*

THE CONCEPT OF FORGIVENESS IS BOTH IMPORTANT AND misunderstood. To forgive and forget is a misnomer. Even in the act of sincere forgiveness it would only be a person suffering from amnesia that would completely forget the initial action of insult. A more realistic view of forgiveness rests in our capacity to put past problems behind us and build a new and better relationship on a fresh foundation. If you are capable of forgiving a person you are acknowledging what originally caused the rift and then recognizing that you no longer feel the burden of pain or anger that once was there. You are moving beyond the pain to a new level of acceptance that allows you to look at the offender with compassion and acceptance. Forgiveness does not mean you lose all memory of what happened. In fact, if you forgot what the offense was you would be incapable of the act of forgiveness because you would have no recall of anything that required it. In forgiving we help two key players. First, the person we forgive may well benefit from the knowledge that the person they wronged has healed. If they are even remotely concerned about the cost of their actions this realization will help them to move on in life and possibly change for the better. This is the nobility of forgiveness as it does open up the doorway for growth in someone else. Likewise, the second beneficiary of forgiveness is the person extending it outwards. Through forgiveness we drop a load of pain that we have carried along with us. Hatred and anger generally punish only the bearer. If we carry the seeds of hate in our spirit we bear a heavy load indeed. Through forgiveness we let go of this burden and open ourselves up to positive energy. In a leadership role you cannot personalize the actions of others.

You will need to know how to forgive if you wish to lead people. Unless you have the compassionate capacity to forgive it will be difficult to work with others. Think about at least one person you bear ill will toward. Then reflect on what burden you are carrying because of those perceptions. Over time, if possible, plan out how you can rid yourself of that emotional burden. Through such thought comes the possibility of both forgiveness and the capacity for growth.

# 43

## *"I shall go just so fast as I think I'm right and the people are ready for the step."*

THERE ARE LEADERS WHO TAKE THE BULL BY THE HORNS AND force change to happen. They career through an organization seemingly intent on tipping over every basket they can reach. The fact that the folks around them are not only resistant but also disoriented by the leader's actions is irrelevant because a certain "vision" must be served. While such situations do exist they will not end well. Change can be taxing. Even well thought out change initiatives will lead some team members to become frustrated. Therefore, it is incumbent upon a leader to carefully assess not only the goal but the state of the troops as well. In military history it is an old axiom that amateurs think about tactics while professionals contemplate logistics. The premise in that wisdom rests upon the very solid ground inherent in the nature of details. It is all well and good to have big ideas but there must be a reasonable and realistic way to operationalize them. God truly does rest in the details. One of the central resources that any organization possesses is the human capital within the system. Simply put—we are only as good as the people we have on board the bus that we are traveling in together. An effective leader needs to know those human capacities and value them. In moving toward a new destination it is essential that the people closest to production have a great deal of input on shaping the route to be taken. It would be an arrogant leader indeed who thought that their own view of any question was superior to that shaped by the people who actually do the work and know the job. As the noted management expert Ken Blanchard once said, "None of us is as smart as all of us." Similarly, there is always the tendency of newly hired leaders to reject past practices and instill new ideas all at once. Such a strategy will lead to alienation and dislocation and rarely has long lasting benefit. No, the key rests in mutually determining a direction and then moving at a reasonable rate. If you as the leader are either too far ahead or behind your troops you will be rejected. Know your people and sustain them as they need to be sustained. This is the essence of stewardship one of the most sacred elements of a leader's credo.

# 44

*"Better give your path to a dog than be bitten by him in contesting for the right. Even killing the dog will not cure the bite."*

I T IS POSSIBLE TO BE RIGHT AND WRONG IN THE SAME BREATH. There are situations that will confront every leader where doing the seemingly "right thing" will result in worse outcomes than either backing away from action or a waiting for an opportunity. The world can be a paradoxical and ironic place. However, that is the way of the world and leaders must learn to be pragmatists. For example, if you are advocating for a certain initiative that will make the organization run more effectively but your boss is not ready to implement it should you push for the "right thing" or bide your time? Only you, in your unique circumstances can answer that question but here is some food for thought. In pushing for something that the system is unready for you may well doom yourself to failure despite the "rightness" of your cause. If people reject a remedy that is good for them it would not be the first time something of that ilk occurred. Another way of looking at this example might be to wait a bit and demonstrate over time why your suggestion is appropriate. You could partially pilot the initiative in your area of responsibility and report back in an objective way on how improvements have materialized. Another approach might be to speak with your boss in private and attempt to ferret out what his or her hesitancy is. If you can get to the heart of your supervisor's opposition you can better strategize how to reasonably overcome it. Without understanding why your boss rejects your proposal you will be poorly armed to advocate for it. Such behavior takes you into unmapped mine fields and will, in all likelihood, leave you no better or worse off than initially. No, the best approach may well be an indirect one that shows how things could be improved without flaunting your entrenched supervisor's opinion. Achieving the "right thing" in the face of opposition can be accomplished in subtle or blunt ways. Fighting over a plan is akin to combat with Mr. Lincoln's aforementioned dog. Even if you "win" you will be bloodied. The bites you receive may or may not heal and the cost is unknown. By deviating from the path a bit to go around the angry and potentially rabid dog you end up where you were headed without having to bandage yourself.

## 45

*"A capacity, and a taste, for reading gives access to whatever has been discovered by others. It is the key, or one of the keys, to the already solved problems. And not only so. It gives a relish, and facility, for successfully pursuing the unsolved ones."*

READING IS A PLEASURE FOR THE AGES. THINK ABOUT THE amazing reality that is contained within the pages of a book. Years ago a writer such as Shakespeare, Louisa May Alcott, Tolstoy, or Dickens sat down and consigned their thoughts onto paper. Over the centuries those words have continued to live and rebound down the halls of people's minds. Books allow the reader to enter into the world of the past and probe for truths uncovered by great minds of bygone ages. People who hate books really reject a significant portion of their own humanity. Thus, a leader who wishes to solve the problems of today or tomorrow can learn a great deal by simply reading about what other people had to say. The power of the printed word is great indeed. When you write something down you take a step that is different than simply thinking about an idea or telling somebody something. It requires conscious effort to sit down and translate your thoughts into readable form. Once on paper ideas are perceived in a different way. You can tell someone about something you have done but it may have a different effect if you take the time to give them the same thoughts in writing. Likewise, if you send someone a note that action has a tremendous influence for good or ill. Be careful what you write down because written documents, far more than the spoken word, have a history of their own. A written report can be evidentiary in a way that is much more palpable then word of mouth testimony.

Similarly, if you wish to document a key happening you had best write down the data or else lose track of it. Leaders should be readers. If a leader is unattached to learning then the question arises as to how deeply they reflect on the worldly matters that are part and parcel of their work? A leader who does not understand the value of books and other print media is one that may well be worthy of suspicion. If you do not treasure the wisdom of the ages how much will you value the ideas of the people around you?

# 46

*"I find quite as much material for a lecture in those points wherein I have failed, as in those wherein I have been moderately successful."*

F AILURE IS A VERY RELATIVE TERM. WHAT APPEARS TO BE A setback can actually be but one step in the longer term successes that you will have. One need only think of the work of scientists such as the Curies who struggled for years in their seemingly fruitless search for radioactive radium. Over a period of years that renowned couple engaged in back breaking labor, apparent futility, and thousands of experiments until they were able to reach their goal. Through persistence and perseverance people can overcome obstacles. Failure is a natural portion of everyone's experiential diet. If you encounter defeat and take it as a lesson to learn from then is it really a failure? Like so many parts of life the way in which we perceive an event to a large extent determines its value for us. If we have a setback and bounce up on our feet to try again then we have grown through the apparent failure. However, if the body blows of life leave us gasping on the ropes we will have difficulty martialing up the levels of resilience that are necessary to be happy and adjusted. Life is impartial in how it metes out the seeming whims of fate. Yet, if you are thorough in your preparation, careful in your planning, prepared with the support of your team, and skilled in your charge you stand a far better chance of succeeding than otherwise. Unfortunately even the most skilled and prepared people meet disaster. If you fall into the category of people facing failure sit back and analyze what you have lost and gained. In "failing" have you truly been defeated or rather temporarily redirected? If you do not perceive a failure as terminal you have every opportunity to recover from it. In fact, it is unlikely that growth in your career and life can effectively occur without setbacks. Does a child learn to walk without falling? Likewise, your role as a leader will involve bumps and bruises. Heal yourself and return to the fray armed with the knowledge afforded you by the rare opportunities inherent in every failure.

# 47

### *"When I have a particular case in hand, I...love to dig up the question by the roots and hold it up and dry it before the fires of the mind."*

T HERE ARE PROBLEMS THAT TAX THE MIND, SPIRIT, AND WILL OF the people attempting to solve them. In those cases it requires the supreme effort of everyone involved to sift through the data and find a way to either make things work or exhaust all reasonable alternatives. The "fires of the mind" that Mr. Lincoln mentions in this quote drawn from his experience as a lawyer are warm indeed. The amount of creativity that goes into finding the solution to complex problems can be astonishing. Those "fires" can warm or consume the person addressing the conundrum. If you take a task as a challenge or puzzle and attack it from a positive direction your work may well become not only bearable but also satisfying. To adopt the opposite approach of wringing your hands over your sad lot in life as epitomized by the problem at hand will result in a self-defeating posture. If you are working in a field that has meaning to you there should be an investment in finding the solutions to issues at hand. As a leader you are charged with either contributing to the resolution of the problem or setting the stage for others to do so. If you find yourself dealing with a taxing issue but also one that stretches you then so much the better. We learn through new experiences. Some of those lessons are painful but even those traumatic events can leave us with a new perspective on who we are and what we do. Let yourself go when momentum takes you. If you look at problems as opportunities to serve and learn then you have a far better chance of solving them. If you are in the flow and moving along at a rapid clip try to remember how that surge feels. In fact, it might well be valuable for you to journal on or reflect about times when you were flowing in a peak way. What was it about those circumstances that allowed you to perform at such a top level? If the "fires of the mind" can be ignited you too will be able to warm yourself by them or gaze at the ever-changing embers as they glow.

## 48

*"I am never easy now, when I am handling a thought, till I have bounded it north and bounded it south, and bounded it east and bounded it west."*

DELIBERATION IS A VIRTUE THAT GOOD LEADERS POSSESS. NOT every decision can be made in a snap second and on the spot. Impulsivity can defeat you if you allow it to do so. Yes, of course, there are times when a quick decision is vital or even life saving. However, normally a leader will have a bit of time to come to a conclusion and act. Well thought out decisions generally supercede in quality those that have been cobbled together in a matter of moments. If you "bound in" your thoughts in a manner that Mr. Lincoln suggests you stand a far greater chance of better serving the needs of the moment than by jumping into the fray without all your intellectual tools available. Through deliberation a leader offers others the gift of wisdom. Further, a leader who takes some time to make a thoughtful decision can consult with other people who may have a great deal to add to the possible solution. There is no shame in seeking out advice when you need it. It is impossible to thoroughly analyze a difficulty if you refuse or are unable to assess it. Despite the pressure that others may place upon you move only when you think the time is ripe to do so. By taking time you act in a prudent and not a reactive manner. Such an approach to problem resolution will help you to form a reputation as a successful and analytical leader. Those colleagues who chide you for taking your time are welcome to their opinion. However, over time, a careful approach to decision making will prevail over one that consistently risks misreading circumstances through haste. As leaders, we are typically not rewarded for how fast we work but rather how well we work.

*"We are not enemies, but friends. We must not be enemies. Though passion may have strained, it must not break our bonds of affection. The mystic chords of memory, stretching from every battlefield, and patriot grave, to every living heart and hearthstone, all over this broad land, will yet swell the chorus of the Union, when again touched as surely as they will be, by the better angels of our nature."*

W HEN ABRAHAM LINCOLN DELIVERED THESE WORDS TO THE congressmen and senators of America in the month just prior to the Confederate attack on Fort Sumter he realized that the nation he loved was falling apart. The bloody reality of internecine civil war was staring him in the face. The nation stood poised on the brink of the abyss and there seemed to be nothing that Mr. Lincoln could do to ameliorate the grievances that had led the people of America there. In these stirring but ultimately futile words Abe Lincoln sought to illustrate the point that people with a shared history, heritage, and understanding should be able to solve problems in a reasonable way. This guidance is as relevant today as it was in March of 1861. In the organization within which you serve there are competing priorities. The interests of labor and management may not always coincide. Customers may favor or reject the efforts of the organization. Different departments within the institution can conceive of themselves as entities unto themselves and not as part of the broader team. People compete for resources and do not always use ethical behavior. When handling these types of potentially destructive events it is important to stop and remember that everyone is part of the team. Even those colleagues who are acting against the goals or directives you have established as a leader are generally not doing so with evil intent. Broad disagreement can occur. Such a situation may be painful to experience. However, you cannot wallow in this pain. Instead, try to seek out solutions through win-win approaches. If you can articulate the opposition's perspective you can better understand it. Reach back into your cognitive toolbox and resurrect the memories that bind you to the people who now stand arrayed against your side. Remember that after the fray is over you will once again be working together. It is difficult to successfully team with people whose hopes and dreams you have tried to squelch. Problems can be solved or at least endured. Take heed from Mr. Lincoln and remember the ties that bind rather than cutting them.

## 50

### *"Fondly do we hope—fervently do we pray—that this mighty scourge of war may speedily pass away."*

AT THE END OF AN INTERMINABLE DAY IT MAY SEEM THAT THERE is not much point to what you do. In fact, on some days you might as well post a sign above your office door for your own viewing pleasure that says, "Abandon all hope, ye who enter." Life can be very difficult at times. Perhaps the greatest solace at such times is that "this too shall pass." In a year will you still be mulling over the issues that appear to be dogging you today? It is generally unlikely that your answer to this question will be "yes." If so you have deeper issues to reflect upon and confront. In such instances take the time to do that contemplative practice and make the changes that will help you to crawl out of the pit of despair that you are in. Seek out professional guidance and assistance as that journey of hope can be a difficult one to take alone. However, in most instances we will not be consumed for long by the seemingly insurmountable ill fortune that we sometimes face. Things pass and that is a fortunate truth. Even when things are going well you need to account for the fact that by and large both good and ill fortune are transitory. Life's journey is cyclical with doses of ups and downs. How we traverse that changing emotional topography determines our satisfaction with life. When things are bad look to your own islands of restitution. In Buddhism there is a concept known as "bells of mindfulness." This concept refers to the stimuli that cue us to think about our happiness and help us to detach from material woe. A "bell of mindfulness" can come in the form of a loved one, a favored activity, wilderness experiences, exercise, or whatever helps you to rejuvenate yourself. Listen to the "bells of mindfulness" and find ways to recoup your strength of will, purpose, mind, body, and spirit. Pain will pass as, in the end, does everything. The pain you feel is real but is it worth your irretrievable present moments to self-impose it in a way that shortchanges you and those who care about you? Let go of the pain and happiness may well follow in its wake.

# 51

## *"This reminds me of the man who murdered his parents and then pleaded for mercy on the grounds that he was an orphan."*

T HERE ARE PEOPLE WHO ARE THEIR OWN WORST ENEMIES. SUCH individuals ramble through life stubbing their proverbial toes left and right. If you happen to have to supervise such a person be aware of their limitations and be sure their irresponsibility does not torpedo the functioning of the team. People who fit this bill may well be unable or unwilling to take responsibility for their actions. Inevitably, the mistakes they make are pawned off on other people, bad luck, the boss, or any number of external factors. Laughable though it may be to see a person childishly trying to skirt responsibility the net effect of these solo flyers is destructive. People who work with or near a person who is irresponsible pay a price for his or her behavior. A team member who is frequently absent for no good reason or who misses meetings will drag down the efficiency of the group. When confronted the slacker will alibi or become defensive about your criticism. Over time, such an individual can become a cancer in an organization. It is incumbent upon the leader to take whatever reasonable steps exist to isolate or remove such a player. If not, then nothing but loss will occur. During the American Civil War over which Mr. Lincoln presided soldiers had a term for such a person. They called him a Jonah and shunned him. A Jonah was a soldier who skipped drill if possible, always appeared on the sick rolls, could never be counted on to take on his share of work, feigned wounds, and generally was a detriment to his company. Jonah's were a problem and they cost people time energy, and even their lives. In your role as a leader you will meet Jonah's. How you handle the most difficult people will to a large extent determine how qualified you are to lead. Be steady and fair in your purpose but always bear in mind that the good of the people you serve is dependent upon reigning in or cutting out a person of this ilk.

# 52

## *"Do I not destroy my enemies when I make them friends?"*

I T IS A NATURAL TENDENCY TO AVOID DIFFICULT PEOPLE. WHY would we seek out people who are tough to be around? Leaders who are charged with making hard decisions may be tormented by individuals who disagree with them. In time it is probable that enemies will develop, as will adherents. In dealing with opponents you can use a variety of strategies. One that might be worthy of attempting is sincerely co-opting your enemies. If you can establish a relationship with an opponent you may both be better served in the future. By reaching out to people who stand in opposition to you it is possible to engage in a form of *détente.* If Richard Nixon, a Cold War warrior of questionable character, could travel to the then USSR and the People's Republic of China in order to thaw relationships you can find the personal strength to reach out to someone who was unpleasant to you. Through such diplomacy you may be able to lessen tension, build bridges, improve the business climate, and simply make human contact with another person who happens to disagree with you. It is easy to depersonalize an enemy. In warfare it is common for opposing forces to simply stop thinking about their enemies as even human. This approach may be the result of the horrors of war or can serve as a psychological defense mechanism that makes the act of killing in combat more palatable to the troops involved. In more sublime business situations an enemy can also assume demonic proportions. Have you ever found yourself characterizing a person who has made your life difficult as irrational, stupid, an idiot, or moronic? You may be underestimating or misunderstanding your opponent. Remember the wise adage that was said by the fictional Don Corleone in Francis Ford Coppola's classic film *The Godfather;* "Keep your friends close, but your enemies closer." Surprisingly, once you get to know your enemy in a civil way you may discover that you have more in common than you ever would have guessed. If so, you have made a friend and lost an enemy. If only life would always work out so well.

# 53

*"In this sad world of ours, sorrow comes to all; and, to the young it comes with bitterest agony, because it takes them unawares."*

IF YOU ARE LEADING A GROUP OF ANY SIZE YOU WILL PROBABLY have people of varying degrees of experience in it. There is most likely a span of ages, a mixture of genders, and varying degrees of professional experience in your teammates. Amongst the group are people who may never have been exposed to the professional "hard knocks" that veterans have had to absorb and rebound from. Less seasoned colleagues may have more difficulty accepting the negative consequences that are part of virtually everyone's career pathway. Bumps in the road may seem deeper and more jarring to a person who has never driven over one before. Therefore, as a leader, you need to take into account the human qualities of each person you work with. Sadness in life and the workplace cannot be ignored or minimized. The staff member who is grieving over a job misstep or a personal loss will not be relieved to hear you tell them, "Well, don't feel too bad; it really isn't a very important moment in your career." If a person is experiencing sorrow simply recognize it and offer the guidance, comfort, and counsel that you have to give. Not to generalize because age does not always bespeak maturity, but, by and large, younger employees will have a harder time coping with their first setbacks than those workers who have "been through the wars." While you need to attend to the emotional needs of all staff members, you may want to pay even closer attention to your newer hires. The early learning sessions that you invest with such a person may stand a greater likelihood of accruing long-term benefit than those you engage in with people who may well be set in their ways. Also, by dedicating some time to supporting and mentoring your less experienced staff members, the more qualified you are to complete the essential personnel decisions that you will be called upon to make regarding new staff.

## 54

*"No, you are mistaken—I am slow to learn and slow to forget...My mind is like a piece of steel, very hard to scratch anything on it and almost impossible after you get it there to rub it out."*

**E**FFECTIVE LEADERS LEARN FROM EXPERIENCE AND RETAIN THE lessons that life affords each and every one of us. Such learning need not infer rigidity or force of habit. No, a flexible mind is a necessary tool in leadership. However, a person who cannot carry with them the sometimes hard teachings of experience is one who may be doomed to repeatedly face the same mistakes, problems, and defeats through poor memory. Lincoln infers that he remembered the lessons that life had scratched upon the surface of his mind. In a typical act of humility Lincoln portrays himself as a slow learner but also one who eventually caught on. In reality, Lincoln was an extremely bright and pragmatic thinker. There is a lesson to be learned in this humble demeanor. Others need not have your abilities and intelligence thrust into their face to appreciate it. Indeed, the leader who constantly pushes his or her capacities to the forefront may well be a person who will be resented or feared by others rather than respected. If you wish to be seen as capable you must demonstrate it in a more subtle yet efficient way. One means of doing so is to internalize the material and personal territory within which you operate. If you learn the ropes of the job as well as how each team member functions, you are a long way down the trail of success. Let those lessons be scratched into the surface of your professional mind. Allow those etchings to sink deep into your consciousness. Such deeper knowledge will stand you in good stead when the time comes to solve problems. You cannot know everything but you need to know the important elements of your work and territory. Those are the lessons that a careful person will learn over time and remember.

# 55

*"Die when I may I want it said of me by those who know me best…that I always plucked a thistle and planted a flower where I thought a flower would grow."*

I T YOU HAVE THE OPPORTUNITY TO DO LASTING GOOD YOU MUST seize it. What sort of leader would bypass a chance to be of service or to help somebody else improve? The answer is a non-leader. If you have a chance to help another person, or a group of people, then it is incumbent upon you to make the best of that opportunity. The planting of a flower is symbolic of many things. The saddened secretary who could be brightened with a kind word or deed is one possible garden spot. The unhappy customer who can have a tiny element of their life improved through courteous service deserves that small act of kindness. The young staff member who has struggled through an ineffective presentation, lesson, or meeting deserves some follow up and moral support in order to realize that all things pass and we all face failure. Through such acts of compassion you accomplish two huge outcomes. First, you extend yourself and potentially assuage the anguish of another person. This is a kind and noble act that should become habit forming. Second, the acts of kindness that you undertake improve the giver as well as the receiver. When we serve others, we serve ourselves as well. Thus, planting flowers where they will grow is a process of improvement that can become contagious. Each person that you model kindness, consideration, and concern for may well plant such seeds of their own as well. Is this not the tone you would like to see established and maintained in your organization? If so, then act in a way that will encourage the planting of such a harvest of compassion.

## 56

*"How hard—Oh how hard it is to die and leave one's country no better than if one had never lived for it!"*

L INCOLN CARRIED WITH HIM A CONCERN FOR HIS NATION THAT was pronounced. As president during a time of extreme national crisis, Lincoln faced unremitting pressures and stress. Lincoln knew that the fate of the unified republic rested upon his shoulders. Yet, throughout his career, Abraham Lincoln emphasized the service element of his work above and beyond the grandeur of his office. For Lincoln his role as national leader was a calling rather than an ego boost. During much of the Civil War Lincoln was unsure as to the outcome of the conflict. The eventual Union victory, which looks to modern eyes as a forgone conclusion due to the inequity of resources, possessed by the North and the South was a very debatable result throughout most of the conflict. There were many moments when the Confederates appeared poised for victory. Of course, in the end, the Union troops marched to victory but not until over 630,000 lives had been lost. In looking at his role and responsibilities Lincoln must have felt overwhelmed at times. Yet, he persevered and spearheaded the Union war effort. There is a supreme lesson to be learned from this pattern of executive behavior. If you are a leader you must accept the responsibilities that go with the position. Each of us leaves a legacy behind. When we leave our jobs, and our life, others will remember us for the things we did and how we behaved. If you wish to leave a positive legacy worthy of respect then your actions must lead people to that set of memories. Through your leadership behavior, the way you treat people, how you handle the needs of others, and the service orientation you establish you mark out the history that will be recalled after your passing. Do you not wish for positive memories? Would you not prefer to be thought of in a loving way? If so, then take the steps today that will guide others to such memories tomorrow. Lead in a way that is worthy of respect and you will be remembered as such.

# 57

## *"All that I am or hope ever to be I got from my mother, God bless her."*

EACH AND EVERY ONE OF US STANDS ON THE SHOULDERS OF others who passed through life before we were even aware of what was happening around us. It is all too easy to forget the deep debts of gratitude that every one of us owes to so many other people. Leaders who lose sight of their debts move toward arrogance. All too many leaders act in ways that make them seem distant power brokers rather than human beings with capabilities. Such people have forgotten their own histories. Each of them was once a babe in arms. As children they were dependent upon the good will of others to survive. Their present positions of power did not simply drop from heaven. Rather, their life was a sequence of interconnected events that melded together to form their present realities. In that tapestry of life a host of other people touched their lives and helped shape them. Think back into your own past. Surely there must have been teachers, relatives, friends, lovers, colleagues, and others who sculpted you in some way. We are social beings living in a social world. We interact with a host of people on a daily basis. Out of that multitude of interactions we engage in the give-and-take of daily life. Over the years that social exchange crafts our habits, style, communication patterns, and approaches to life's drama. The leader who forgets all the steps that led to his or her current position is actually sleepwalking through life. We must acknowledge the important parts that other people have played, and continue to play, in our individual lives. Naturally, our parents may stand out as primary elements in our early development. But that is not always true. Every person has had a unique life. That uniqueness extends to relationships inclusive of their interactions with their parents. What is important is that

82

through reflection each of us comes to realize that who we are and what we do is the result of a vast set of human interactions and relationships. If we forget the importance of other people's roles in our life we lose a vital part of our own history. If you wish to lead then you need to remember why you act the way you do. Through acknowledging our past debts we set the stage for seeing the future much more clearly than if we ignore our history.

# 58

## *"Let us have faith that right makes might; and in that faith, let us, to the end, dare to do our duty, as we understand it."*

I F YOU HAVE ANY HOPES OF BEING AN EFFECTIVE LEADER YOU must face the reality that your strength, will, values, and character will be tested. Leaders face tough decisions with great regularity. There will be temptations in your career. In some instances you will be tempted to look the other way in order to avoid an unpleasant situation. Some battles may appear to be unwinable even though you know that justice is on your side. You will be placed in the crucible of power and ground down by the pestle of life. However, despite the many challenges that go with being a leader, you can thrive in that environment. A key resides in your understanding what your core values are. If you have reflected upon your beliefs, and acted in an ethical way during your career, you can look back with humble & deserving pride at your accomplishments. Conversely, if you have vacillated in your beliefs, acted in a way that avoided responsibility whenever possible, or ignored the moral requirements of your job you will be a failure. Some failures are hard to recognize. I have had the opportunity to work with people who ascended to powerful and lucrative positions with seemingly no capability to handle the responsibilities given to them. These people moved on to even more powerful positions or retired with comfortable pensions but really left negative legacies behind them. Perhaps, over time, these individuals will be troubled in their sleep over the things they did or did not do. I have no way of knowing what their respective consciences tell them in their honest moments of self-analysis. However, what I can say is that I have no desire to look back on my leadership career and feel humiliated over the incongruence that could exist between what I believe and what I did as a leader. If you wish to feel some sense of accomplishment and service in your leadership career then you must first think through why you wish to be a leader. Then, you must act in accordance with your core values and adjust your behavior along the way in light of changing circumstances. But, those adjustments cannot compromise what you believe in or you will ultimately fail. Your failure may be subtle and unnoticed by many, but you will recognize it and recount it to yourself over the years.

# 59

## *"I have always wanted to deal with everyone I meet candidly and honestly. If I have made any assertion not warranted by facts, and it is pointed out to me, I will withdraw it cheerfully."*

E VERYONE MAKES MISTAKES. A STRONG PERSON REALIZES THAT it is far better to acknowledge an error than to push ahead as if nothing went wrong. In demonstrating the ability to ferret out your own failures or errors of judgment, and then correct them openly, a leader models a flexible mindset that will gain supporters rather than lose them. It requires a secure sense of self to admit mistakes. However, the alternatives are far worse than any opprobrium that may descend upon a person who owns up to problems rather than covering them up. People know when things are going well and when they are not. There are many leaders who will cloak failure with the raiment of brilliant success. If the mistakes of the leader become too apparent then he or she will scapegoat another person and thereby remain above the fray. Toadies and other minions will bobble their heads as they shake in their boots while simultaneously fawning their way into the good graces of this type of ego-driven leader. In the long haul this type of behavior cannot be the source of growth and development within a system. Conversely, this sort of person at the head will almost assure such a system of at best stuttering progress and at worst a crushing failure. On the other hand, it is the cogent leader who can look error in the face and see a reflection of themselves and their plans that must be acknowledged and modified. Like Mr. Lincoln, the flexible mind linked to an openness of character will stand both a leader and his or her teammates in good stead.

## <u>60</u>

*"A man watches his pear-tree day after day, impatient for the ripening of the fruit. Let him attempt to force the process and he may spoil both fruit and tree. But let him patiently wait, and the ripe pear at length falls into his lap."*

I F YOU CHOOSE TO LEAD PEOPLE YOU WILL EXPERIENCE MOMENTS of rejection, misrepresentation, and regret. Leading is a challenge even in the best of times. When any sort of fiscal or interpersonal crisis occurs in a system then the leader will inherit even more dissonance. When people are stressed they may react in an abrasive way. The pressures of the job may become compounded by additional responsibilities, longer hours, and changes that folks can perceive as negative. Leading requires a somewhat thick skin. It is an immature leader that expects things to always be rosy. Leaders must gird themselves for the darker days within which people are tough to deal with. It is the hard days that make or break a leader. If you can lead when things go sour then you will be capable of mastering the ship of state in easier times. Indeed, it can be said that a leader who can cope with a crisis can set the stage for days of calm. If you handle the tough decisions, circumstances, and problems you will be aligned with the planets to succeed in the long run. A leader who can weather these periodic and inevitable storms will gain respect from the people around them. They will be seen as a problem solver and a person who can be relied upon to come through in the clutch. Problems and disagreements cannot overwhelm a leader. Likewise, the actions of others should not be personalized. If you bury the hatchet of resentment rather than bearing long term grudges you set the stage for growth. Conversely, if you carry the seeds of anger and personal animosity in your spirit they will fester and overwhelm you. The harmony of your spirit and the system you lead depend upon your capacity to handle tough situations productively and in ways that enhance union rather than division. A leader who can maintain calmness and forgive transgressions is a mature soul who will prosper.

# 61

*"The true rule, in determining to embrace or reject any thing, is not whether it has any evil in it; but whether it has more of evil than good. There are few things wholly evil or wholly good."*

P EOPLE OFTEN GET IN TROUBLE WHEN THEY VIEW THE WORLD through lenses of absolutism. It can be very easy to see issues in strands of black and white. If life were only so simple there would be no difficulty in universally determining right from wrong. All problems would have manifest solutions. All in all, the world would be a simple place where contrasting forces of good and evil could be easily determined. In reality, life is far from simple. Problems sneak up on you. Solutions can be hard to come by. In many instances the solution to one problem bears the seeds of future difficulties. Good and evil are often hard to discriminate from one another. People who appear well intended may be among your secret opponents. Similarly, a person or group that remains reticent may be on the right side but reserved in nature. The world is a jumble of interconnected problems and solutions that act to complement one another. An effective leader realizes that generally his or her actions will not result in immaculate goodness or the darkest evil. In many cases leaders are forced to find reasonable compromises to problems. Factors such as negotiation, give-and-take, and compromise are all vital survival skills for an effective leader. While a strong and well-intended leader cannot compromise essential core values it is necessary to merge differing perspectives in complex situations. If you deal in absolutes you can be sure of one ultimate result—you will fail. Conversely, if you are capable of weighing the impact of varied and flawed alternatives, you may have the capacity for mediation that is required of all great leaders.

## 62

### *"The habit of uselessly wasting time is the whole difficulty; and it is vastly important...that you should break this habit."*

**I**F YOU WISH TO LEAD YOU WILL NEED TO DEVELOP EFFECTIVE time management skills. A leader who is disorganized and wastes time is a leader who will be drowned by the day-to-day requirements of the job. It is a rare leadership assignment indeed that will not offer a taxing schedule of work. Therefore, the life of a leader is one that requires top-flight time management. There are many ways to augment your ability to manage time. Planners, palm pilots, computerized scheduling, list making, and any number of interventions can help a leader to make the best possible use of time. Whatever method you choose be sure to realize that time is the ultimate non-renewable resource. Each of us has only so many sands to flow through the personal hourglasses of our lives. Once that allotment of time is over we pass out of this mortal world. Therefore, is it not prudent to take whatever actions we can to make the best use of the time we have been given? In Shakespeare's *Richard II* the imprisoned and doomed monarch laments, "I have wasted time, and now doth time waste me." This sad eulogy is a stark one & as such should be taken to heart. If you wish to be effective as a leader you must harness time. Further, if you wish to be able to achieve a healthy life balance inclusive of work, family, hobbies, and other important elements then you had better become proficient at managing your time. People who squander this elemental resource may someday look back and wonder where their lives went. What a sad commentary and possibility that scenario is. Thus, take charge of your schedule and, in so doing, find the time necessary to be a well organized leader and a balanced person.

# 63

## *"All creation is a mine, and every man, a miner."*

E ACH OF US HAS A CREATIVE AND INVESTIGATIVE SPIRIT. EVERY person has value. It is incumbent upon a leader to discover the value of all staff members who work with them. In some instances the mining of human value can be a tough task indeed. Some people are not fully aware of the values, talents, and achievements that they encompass. It is a skilled leader who can help individuals and groups unearth the traits that they possess but are unaware of. Of course, not every person is well matched with his or her assignment. There are times when the mining or evaluation process will find people wanting. In such situations it is essential that the leader take the correct and humane steps necessary to help or replace that person. A leader does no one a kindness by maintaining ill-suited people in positions that are important. Everything that we do or strive to accomplish is an act of creation. The world is a vast treasure trove of possibilities. If we strive to create a system within which the search for creative outcomes is appreciated we take huge steps toward crafting an effective workplace. Part of that endeavor is making sure that creative ideas are encouraged. Likewise, each employee should be congratulated for the fine steps they take in their daily work. In supporting the successes of others we ingrain a belief in achievement. Similarly, in honestly offering feedback that is critical in a decent and private way we allow for growth as well. Men and women who lead must be the miners that Lincoln alludes to in this reference. Mining can be hard, sweaty, and grinding work. However, a miner can reveal gemstones, gold, and silver. In the workplace these precious elements take the form of productivity, teamwork, and achievement. Take the time to recognize these vital accomplishments as you move the earth of life from place to place.

## 64

*"What I cannot do, of course I will not do; but it may as well be understood, once for all, that I shall not surrender this game leaving any available card unplayed."*

**E**FFECTIVE LEADERS REALIZE THAT THEY MUST PRODUCE WHEN times get tough. If you wish to lead people they must understand that you will make every reasonable effort to support what is right with all your powers. Of course, exerting maximum effort in pursuit of questionable goals or unwinable contests is an act of futility. A leader must be able to discern what is reasonable and what is not. Yet, if a leader wishes to be respected he or she must use all ethical cards available to secure success. If you act in a way that communicates defeatism people will give up on following you. If you act in a way that models compromise of principle you will be seen as unprincipled. Leaders who give up without much of an effort are justly viewed as weak. How successful can and should you be if you cannot be counted upon to fight the good fight on behalf of truth? In Lincoln's day issues that appeared overwhelming in nature confronted him. President Lincoln faced the very disintegration of the nation he loved and served. On a daily basis President Lincoln was forced to make tough decisions, negotiate compromises, face public scorn, and do battle with ideologues and mean spirited people. Throughout that taxing time Lincoln remained true to the pragmatics and beliefs that had vaulted him into the presidency. Even in times of crisis, and perhaps then even more so than in calmer moments, a leader must support the principles that are guiding lights. To fail to do so is to fail at the very heart of leadership.

# 65

*"I have found that when one is embarrassed, usually the shortest way to get through with it is to quit talking about it or thinking about it, and go at something else."*

**E**VERYONE MAKES MISTAKES. SOME OF THOSE MISTAKES CAN BE very embarrassing and stress inducing. There will be times when it is hard to leave the office because you know people are judging you based upon a recent error. There will be hard nights when you toss and turn in your sleeplessness and engage in thought attacks upon yourself for your transgressions. Yet, in the long run, it is essential that you put those mistakes behind you and move on to something else. Mistakes are temporary defeats that can lead to future victories. In erring today we plant the seeds for future improvement. If you make a mistake acknowledge it and learn from the events. An error in judgment can usually be corrected. You will magnify your problems if you do not own up to what has happened and move ahead. It is also important to reflect on what the mistake was all about. In reflectively looking at your own behavior you set the stage for improvement. Your improvement as a decision maker will, in turn, enhance the capacities of the system within which you work. However, there is a difference between reflection and maudlin dwelling. Of course, your initial reaction to an error will be to process it and even fixate upon it. If you find yourself recycling your behavior and creating anxiety—stop that process cold. Think about what you are doing to yourself and consciously choose to put those repetitive and self-damaging thoughts behind you. When you are better able to focus productively upon the chain-of-events then you will have the capacity for reflection. In reflection you can rethink what happened and what could or should have occurred. These reflective moments are a roadmap for future improvement. In Mr. Lincoln's time he had the opportunity to ponder disastrous military defeats, rebellions within his own party, ambitious underlings who subverted his decisions, poor generalship that cost tens of thousands of lives, and the raging reality of civil war. He lost many nights sleep pondering the potentially terrible fate that his nation faced. But, he handled those immense problems and helped set the stage for victory. In your own leadership life you will also face the test of failure. How you handle that grim visaged foe will determine whether or not you progress to a more mature phase of leadership.

# 66

## *"The severest justice may not always be the best policy."*

WITH SUPERVISION COMES THE ROLE OF EVALUATION. PEOPLE are imperfect and will make mistakes. Sometimes staff members will act in ways that are unbelievably immature, unprofessional, and short sighted. In other instances people cannot be maintained in their present job because they are unable to achieve. In dealing with the transgressions of colleagues a leader establishes his or her reputation for personnel judgment. Some leaders avert their eyes and refuse to see the mistakes that employees make. They falsely believe that in ignoring problems they will disappear. In reality, a leader who follows this pathway of ignorance will not only lose credibility but will also make the system weaker. Conversely, a leader who remorselessly punishes people for their mistakes will soon become a feared person but not necessarily a respected one. In handling people's mistakes you need to treat them in the way you would want to be treated in that situation if the tables were turned. Dictatorial and draconian leaders soon earn a reputation for remorselessness. Fear is not a prime motivator. People who work in fear of the consequences for making mistakes will probably make more of them. Communication in such a system will become closed. People will refrain from going to such a dictator with information and ideas for fear of the negativity that might descend upon them. Dictatorships eventually fall. If you treat other people poorly that negative karma will rebound back to you. Is that the energy that you wish to share in the world? If you have to handle a difficult personnel situation do so with integrity. Do not personalize your feedback. Talk to the person with reason and not with anger. Remember that most mistakes can be learned from. Think back to your own experiences with past supervisors. If you can remember terrible ways in which you were treated do not recreate them yourself and then, in turn, impose them upon others. We can work through most problems together and do so with dignity & respect. That is why the bitterest medicine of judgment should only be ladled out on rare occasions when it will cure and not kill the recipient.

# 67

## *"Fellow-citizens, we cannot escape history."*

SOMETIMES PEOPLE ACT AS IF THERE WAS NO SUCH THING AS history. New leaders descend upon an organization. They bring with them preconceived notions of what their new system should look like. Change initiatives are launched. Task forces and committees are formed. Administrative teams are reorganized or restructured. New flow charts of duties and responsibilities are crafted and circulated. Lines of responsibility are erased and redrawn. Slogans are bandied about. New vision statements are developed. Strategic planning initiatives are commenced and pushed ahead. However, in all too many cases, all of these activities are done in a way that ignores the cultural history of the organization. Each person and every system has a history. By ignoring those personal and systemic histories new leaders run an enormous risk of failure. For example, how effectively can you restructure a group that you have not taken the time to analyze? In developing a new vision statement or strategic plan, how well received will that work be if your system has repeatedly undertaken such initiatives and consistently ignored the dictums established? Can a new leader who ignores the history of a system actually intelligently act to change it? Through taking some time to learn at least the surface elements of a system's cultural history a leader exercises patience, maturity, and a pragmatic demeanor. If you are moving into a new leadership role take the time necessary to analyze how things work before you begin to muck about with change. One of the worst things that leaders can do is to blindly alter things in a system without fully understanding the implications of change. Every system has an interconnected ecology of its own. As in the natural world, the elimination of a species, the draining of a wetland, or the cutting down of a rainforest has implications that stretch out like the ripples in a pond. Those ripples will circle out to distant shores and exert an effect that is unforeseen. Take your time when you are thinking about changes. Learn from stakeholders what attitudes and past practices have been. In learning the lessons of history we behave in a thoughtful manner. In ignoring the history of the place you work you run the risk of rehashing past mistakes and cementing the institutional cynicism that can take root in such a rudderless organization. You cannot escape history—but you can learn from it.

# 68

## *"No man who has resolved to make the most of himself can spare time for personal contention"*

**T**HERE ARE LEADERS WHO DROP EVERYTHING TO GET EVEN WITH someone else. Such people are typically combative and argumentative. They will sacrifice the good of the organization for vengeance sake. Personal agendas are preeminent for such a person. In my own life as a leader I have had the opportunity to work for such people. What you find in such a circumstance is that people who fawn upon the leader's ego will advance. Such toadyism is rewarded by decent treatment, professional advancement, and security of a sort. However, that security and progress is bought at a huge cost. Under a leader who acts in this shortsighted and cruel manner people who choose to stand with him or her sacrifice their professional soul. People who know what they are doing will eventually disrespect them. Likewise, negative leaders generally do not remain in an organization for too long a time. They create so much institutional and inter-personal destruction that they have to move on. Once they are gone, their past toadies and minions are left unprotected and unadorned. Under a new regime their past alliances may come back to haunt them. Thus, when working under a negative leader who thrives on dominance you must remain true to your core values. Of course, such a pathway may result in conflict if those values do not exactly coincide with the leader's. When faced with a destructive superior who brooks no debate you cannot regress into the cocoon of being a "yes-person." Try to avoid confrontations if possible but refrain from violating your professional ethics. Go underground if you can and act in a professional but unobtrusive manner. If things become unbearable look for an internal or external job change. Whatever you decide to do remember that if you overtly compromise what you believe in to assuage a corrupt and corrupting leader you become what you hate. In Nazi Germany there were many people who chose to ignore what was happening to the Jews. While those people did not directly participate in the Holocaust they aided it through their indifference and fear. Do you want your legacy to be that your only defense once the dictator has fallen is that you really did not know how bad things were? In handling such a mean spirited superior we also learn valuable lessons for our own leadership practices. Do not impose upon others the cruelties that have been handed down to you. There really is no time for personal agendas and battles. Time is everything and it should be used in the pursuit of positive achievements & relationships and not on petty demagoguery.

# 69

## *"Determine that the thing can and shall be done, and then we shall find the way."*

**W**HEN CONFRONTED WITH PROBLEMS, GROUPS OF PEOPLE COME up with solutions. Once a solution has been determined it is the leader's responsibility to secure the necessary resources to accomplish the outcome. Of course, no single person will derive all the resources needed to work a problem. Every participant in the process of crafting a solution exerts an influence upon the result. The human resources that each individual possesses become part of the solution. There is a wonderful concept know as "synergy."

This term refers to the increased power that derives from the combination of elements. In a synergistic view of the world the sum of a group's energy is greater than the total of its individual components. In the real world of leadership this synergistic perspective comes into play when thinking about how powerful an effective team can be. If you take a few moments to think about great teams that you have been a part of you will be surprised at how synergistic they were. A great team is better than the individual talents of its members. Each team member brings unique gifts to the group. Once shared, those separate talents merge into a unified whole that is amazing. Such teams can tackle problems that its individual members would have faltered in the face of. Thus, in determining what resources are necessary to undertake a solution, never underestimate the power that is latent and manifest in the teams you build. Also, maintain a realistic but positive attitude about the likelihood of success. No one wants to follow a leader who behaves like a sad sack or who mimics Eyore from *Winnie the Pooh.* Be upbeat and take the practical steps you can to secure resources. If you encounter problems in securing what is needed come back to the team and use the synergy of the group to determine potential adjustments or alternatives. Remember, in undertaking a major initiative you are not alone. Through the energy of your teammates you can accomplish goals that you alone would fail to achieve. Use the resources that you have to generate even more quality than you can imagine.

# 70

*I shall try to correct errors when shown to be errors; and I shall adopt new views so fast as they shall appear to be true views."*

A STUBBORN LEADER IS A WEAK ONE. LEADERS WHO ARE unbending will break. The string of opinion that an unchangeable leader draws tight will snap. Errors un-admitted to can metastasize into deadly growths. If you wish to be an effective and productive leader you must be flexible. Times and people change. If you retain an unchanging view of the world you run the risk of being left in the wake of history. Having the ability to think in flexible ways is a mark of intelligence. Rigid thinkers see the world through a very narrow set of blinders. They sometimes fear change and resist new ideas. In resisting the new they hang on to what is familiar to them. While this may be a very understandable human action it is also one that will doom the leader and his or her colleagues to vulnerability. In the private sector an absence of flexibility can result in being consumed by the marketplace. In the public sector leaders who are unable to handle new technologies, changing legal structures, altered demographics, or the way of the world will falter. In flexibility, grounded upon principle, we have a tool for coping with change. A flexible leader is not without core values. He or she operates from a perspective that is consistent and ethical. However, when confronted with novel circumstances, a leader with a flexible mindset can better cope with the unpredicted than one who is very limited in options. Flexible people are better prepared than dogmatists to solve problems. If you see the world unilaterally you will conflict with anyone who has a different view. Conversely, if you are open to reasonable influence you can harness differences and make things better. In flexibility lies the hope of resolution and the means to the ends of reasoned progress.

# 71

## *It is man's duty to improve not only his own condition, but to assist in ameliorating mankind. "*

**E**VERY DAY THAT WE GO TO WORK WE ARE GIVEN THE GIFT OF opportunity. On a daily basis we can help other people. This is a wondrous gift. Think about the possibilities given to each of us to help others. In a leadership capacity a person can expand the opportunities to assist others. Every leader has the potential for great good. In helping other people to, in turn, treat their clients with compassion, care, kindness, and empathy we develop an organization that is people-centered. It is everyone's responsibility to make the world a better place. In modeling the values that we feel are decent and growth-oriented a leader takes the first step in that process. Leadership is not about power and control. It is about achievement, responsibility, and service. Leaders are servants to those with whom they work. While they do have certain influence upon the tide of events they cannot become so egotistical as to believe that they alone are worthwhile. Good leaders realize that the goals of their systems must rest upon pro-social outcomes. If your daily actions do not build toward the betterment of others what is the real purpose of your work? Every day that you go to work seek out opportunities to be of service. In this simple yet sublime way you will be part of the solution and not the problem.

# 72

## *"I am for those means which will give the greatest good to the greatest number."*

**A** LEADER IS A CARETAKER IN CHARGE OF THE WELFARE OF others. As such, he or she must always assess the results that will flow from action or inaction. If you are faced with a decision there will be attendant results. Every action changes things in some way. Hopefully the changes caused by your actions will be far more positive than negative. However, there is a balance in life. Things do not always move in a positive direction. Thus, when making decisions you must make a cost benefit analysis. If you are forced to make a decision that will exact a cost from some person or group you must be sure that the concomitant benefits are great. If at all possible engage in win/win decision-making. In such a scenario the changes wrought by your actions will create an atmosphere for general good. In reality, life is not always so benevolent. In making decisions we must always balance the greater good. If, for example, your actions as a leader cost some people their jobs while setting the stage for the survival of your organization you need to assess more than simply the bottom line. In making such a change you will cause stress for those employees who lose their job. On the other hand, inaction could result in the destruction of your system. In the latter case potentially all employees of the firm would be out of work. Faced with such a painful choice a leader must exhaust all options and then implement the plan that assures the greatest good for the most people. This type of decision-making should never unilaterally ignore the needs of minority elements in a given circumstance. The minority body can exert pressure and come up with ideas that are better than your own. In making such wrenching decisions take the time you have available to you to fully analyze all perspectives. Once you have all the information you can reasonably expect to receive, then go ahead and make the tough call that you are confronted with. If you base your decision on the greater good you stand a far better chance of carrying out a difficult assignment in the most decent way possible. You may not be uniformly loved for your actions but you will be acting in an ethical way.

# 73

## *"Government of the people, by the people, for the people, shall not perish from the Earth."*

I N PRESIDENT LINCOLN'S DAY THE VERY FATE OF THE AMERICAN republic hung in the balance. In the spring of 1861 when the Confederacy was born and shots were fired on Fort Sumter it was quite probable that the American nation would fragment into two, and possibly more, constituent parts. For Lincoln, as well as all unionists across the land, that probability was unacceptable. In their eyes the American experiment in democracy represented not only a national treasure but also a beacon of freedom for the people of the world. Lincoln truly believed in the concepts of emancipation, democracy, and civil liberties. Ironically, as a president presiding during a civil war Mr. Lincoln enacted laws that sharply circumscribed individual liberties. However, despite the necessity of delimiting some constitutional freedoms President Lincoln gave every ounce of personal effort to wage a successful campaign against what he viewed as the forces of privilege, slavery, and rebellion. In your leadership role you will be vested with a certain level of authority. There will be times when you will need to use your authority in ways that will be unpopular. But, if you consistently act in a way that is despotic you will be a lonely and unsuccessful person. In making high stakes decisions you will be well advised to involve relevant parties in the process. While consensus decisions are not always possible they are generally stronger and more universally accepted than unilateral ones. Democratic processes are fragile and can be snuffed out with very little effort. Yet, once gone what viable form of governance is left behind? If you wish to lead than take the time to listen. In making decisions consult stakeholders and act in concert with the people you value. In working collaboratively you demonstrate the confidence that effective leaders must have while simultaneously behaving in a reasonable manner.

# 74

*"If the end brings me out all right, what is said against me won't amount to anything. If the end brings me out wrong, ten angels swearing I was right would make no difference."*

U SUALLY LEADERS ARE EVALUATED BASED UPON RESULTS. IF you can consistently deliver the desired outcome you will be seen as a proficient leader. Reputation is a part of leadership. The way you behave and carry yourself will go a long way toward crafting the image that others will identify with you. If you can be approachable, calm in crisis situations, able to solve problems, and fair then people will adjudge you to be the type of person they would willingly place confidence in. One element of reputation that some leaders confuse themselves with is praise. Most people have an innate desire to receive positive feedback. It feels good to have someone acknowledge your hard work and perseverance. A kind word from another person goes a long way toward making for a good day. But, if your pursuit of praise supercedes your focus on job productivity then you will run afoul of your own needs. You may have worked with administrators who were sucked into the trap of yearning for good feelings. Such a leader may lose sight of the faults in a person who uses praise to worm their way into his or her good graces. There will be times when people will unjustly criticize leaders. If the hunt for praise is a dominant factor in a leader's life he or she will ultimately achieve frustration rather than success. If you refuse to make tough and somewhat unpopular decisions because of what people will think of you, then your leadership may be disabled. Likewise, if you make an unpopular decision and find out that you were wrong, the best course of action is to change direction gracefully. Praise and blame are facts of life. As a leader you certainly need to consider them as aspects of decision-making.

But, in the long run, you must act based upon principle regardless of the way people think of you. Eventually your actions will be judged by standards of productivity and not the subjective opinions of people who may know very little about the reality of the situation you are dealing with.

## 75

*"I have had so many evidences of His direction, so many instances when I have been controlled by some other power than my own will, that I cannot doubt that this power comes from above."*

T HERE HAS BEEN A FAIR AMOUNT OF DEBATE REGARDING Abraham Lincoln's religious faith. There are scholars who claim that Lincoln was a very religious man who frequently read from the Bible. If you ever visit Springfield, Illinois you can tour the church in the downtown area where the Lincolns attended worship. On the other hand, there are some historians who question Mr. Lincoln's religious beliefs. These researchers view Lincoln as more of a rationalist who saw God in a way that did not quite fit into the containments of traditional Christian faith. In Lincoln's writings, as evidenced by this quotation, there are frequent references to the divine forces that influence life. In leadership there should be some sense that all things pass. Leaders certainly need not be part of a traditional or non-traditional religious faith. There are many wonderful leaders who openly question the tenets of organized religion. Conversely, most effective leaders have some form of spirituality to them that serves as a moral compass. Spirituality does not directly correlate to religion. A person can be spiritual without believing in God, Allah, the principles of Buddhism, or the Taoist creed. Spirituality bespeaks an acknowledgement of moral principles that place an emphasis on concepts such as the common good, service to others, a valuing of life, and an understanding of the interconnectedness of all sentient beings. A leader who has a belief system that acknowledges the involvement of amazing and transcendent forces in life may well feel more grounded in tough times than a person who is vacant in terms of values. If we realize that each of us is both unique and transitory then it becomes easier to place problems in perspective. If you are facing a challenging time in your life there should be some solace in the realization that many other people across the ages have faced similar issues and coped with them. If you can acknowledge your own unimportance you can then put your stresses in order. A belief in forces greater than yourself is a tonic for creeping egotism. Who can stand in the sight of the natural wonders of the world and think that their business concerns are universal and permanent in importance?

# 76

## *"Too often we read only of successful experiments in science and philosophy, whereas if the history of failure and defeat was included there would be a saving of brain work as well as time."*

**P**EOPLE REVEL IN SUCCESS AND LEAVE FAILURE AS AN abandoned orphan. Victory has many fathers but defeat is a disdained isolate. In reality, as history shows, some of the most effective leaders are those who faced dire circumstances and eventually prevailed. In Mr. Lincoln's case electoral defeat, public scorn, disparagement by cabinet officers, media ridicule, and domestic disturbance all marked him as a person who was underestimated for decades. Those who worked closely with Abraham Lincoln realized his great capacities. But those followers were outnumbered on occasion by the many citizens who rebuked him for his own and other's failures. Of course history now reckons Lincoln to be among the finest of America's leaders. Lincoln learned valuable lessons from his defeats. Through accepting the bitter draft that defeat can be and learning from its aftertaste, Mr. Lincoln modeled the approach that transforms setbacks into valuable lessons. If you lead you will face defeat. You have two choices when handling professional or personal setbacks. On the one hand you can honor the natural instincts that often overwhelm a defeated leader and ignore what has happened. It is easy to rationalize a loss and put it out of your mind. In this way we set ourselves up for a repeat performance. A person who does not process a defeat is probably going to blunder into the same set of circumstances in the future. Unexamined history will become future reality. Conversely, people can learn the lessons of history and arm themselves for improvement. In 1861 Ulysses S. Grant found it difficult to secure any sort of meaningful military commission. His poor reputation due to loneliness and drinking when he served in the army prior to the Civil War had tarnished his image. A few short years later Grant was the supreme commander of the Federal Army and the man who orchestrated the Union's military victory. Grant accomplished this amazing comeback by realizing his shortcomings and dealing with them. He faced numerous defeats in the 1864 Overland Campaign in Virginia. But, through dogged perseverance and pragmatism he wore down the army of General Lee and crushed it. You can learn from your past. In that learning lie some of the deepest lessons you will need to master not only for professional success but also to live a life of balanced happiness.

# 77

## *"The world shall know that I will keep my faith to friends and enemies, come what will."*

**I**F PEOPLE KNOW THEY CAN DEPEND ON YOU AND TRUST YOUR word you will probably be a successful leader. Honestly standing by colleagues when they need support is a surefire way to harvest loyalty. There will be times when you will need to support someone publicly and then offer criticism to them in private. That is a very reasonable approach to adopt as it guarantees integrity without sacrificing temperance. Whatever the circumstance you must behave in an honest and ethical manner. This applies not only to your fans but also to your opponents. In your leadership career you will get to know people who consistently test or oppose you. Never underestimate the capacities of your opponent. That pathway leads to surprise, confusion, and potential disaster. Always admire your opponents and try to take their perspective. If you can successfully see things through your opponent's eyes you may discover the weaknesses in your own stance. Opponents who you come to understand can even become honored friends over time. The keynote factor here is that you must approach opponents in an honest and consistent way. If you work honestly with someone who disagrees with you they should at least respect you. Out of respect and trust come the seeds for settlement of outstanding differences. In any case, ingrain honesty in your doings. If you are honest you never have to have the amazing memory that liars require. In truth lies the potential for compromise. Through compromise comes the possibility of peace.

# 78

## *"Those who deny freedom to others deserve it not for themselves."*

**H**AVE YOU EVER WORKED FOR A PERSON WHO WAS A TYRANT? If you have then you will realize how oppressive that experience can be. Tyrants see themselves as omnipotent. They place great value upon their opinions, accomplishments, and power. Indeed, much of what tyrants do is based upon the dual pillars of power and control. Actions will be taken that make no programmatic sense merely because it is the whim of the leader. In other instances a tyrant will act in counterproductive ways simply because he or she can do so. In a tyranny, by definition, nobody is free except the leader. Those individuals who stand up to the tyrant will pay a price. The loss of a job in the face of a tyrant is a possibility. Likewise, tyrants can make life miserable for those subordinates they choose to poke at with their scepter. In Lincoln's day-and-age tyranny took its most pronounced form in the slave owning south. There, some people were considered mere chattel. African-Americans were bought, sold, and tormented at their master's whim. For Lincoln, the southern aristocrats who dominated both the Antebellum Southland and the pre-war Federal Government were unfit for freedom. At times Mr. Lincoln could adopt a writing style similar to the Old Testament books that he sometimes read. While Lincoln certainly did not literally wish to enslave the former slaveholders, he was sincere in his distaste for the practice of slavery and its advocates. If you wish to be free yourself, you cannot impose slavery upon others. The tyrannical leader who stifles everyone around him or her in pursuit of self-aggrandizement is an evil force. If you wish to be a respected leader then always avert from this style of management. There will be times when you have to make decisions that stand in opposition to common beliefs held by others. However, you cannot run your organization like a police state or you will flounder. Eventually people rebel against tyranny. That rebellion can take overt and covert forms. But, rest assured that if you are a tyrant some form of guerrilla or open war will dog your heels. Through dictatorship lies a pathway to suffering. Through collaboration comes the harvest of sharing and progress.

# 79

*"My friends—No one, not in my situation, can appreciate my feeling of sadness at this parting."*

IF YOU WISH TO BE A LEADER YOU WILL PROBABLY HAVE TO make career decisions that involve change and movement. Very few people rise to a leadership position in the organization that they start their careers in. Even fewer individuals spend their entire career in one system. Therefore, if you wish to advance your career into the field of leadership you have chosen you will have to change jobs. We live in an age when more and more people are transitioning across multiple jobs in their careers & the standards of loyalty and longevity that earlier generations cherished have changed. In this era it is unlikely that an effective leader will stay in a given post for more than five years. Those people who persevere and establish long-term leadership commitments in a given post are very rare. Thus, if advancement and leadership services are your goals—you will be moving on. If you are a person who is fit to lead others you are also an individual who connects to the colleagues around you. A positive leader is a person-centered individual. That sort of person will establish relationships of value in their workplace. If you connect with people it is painful to leave them in pursuit of new jobs. There is sadness in all partings. It would be a superficial person indeed who could come into a work situation and not feel the tug of emotion when the time comes to move on. But, time and circumstance do move ahead. Even when you depart from a system you leave behind the trace elements of legacy & memory. If you have led well and decently your legacy will be in the form of the positive memories that trail behind you. Likewise, within yourself, you are a changed person because of the contacts you have made. Every action, relationship, and experience changes who we are. Similarly, each of us is a change agent in the lives of those people we encounter in life's journey. In moving on we leave people, places, and things behind but we also carry them with us. When Mr. Lincoln spoke these words to people gathered in Springfield, Illinois he was heading to Washington and a weight of problems that was incalculable. Lincoln forged ahead and achieved great things at great cost. In your life moving on will be a factor you will have to deal with. In forging ahead do not lose sight of the people you have known and the shoulders you have stood on to get a better view.

# 80

*"My countrymen, one and all, think calmly and well, upon this whole subject. Nothing valuable can be lost by taking time."*

**I**F YOU HAVE TO MAKE MAJOR DECISIONS THERE IS NO HARM, AND much to commend itself, in taking time. All too often leaders feel that they must rush to a decision. There are far too many leaders who commit the cardinal sin of leaping before they look. Down that pathway can lay suffering otherwise averted through reflection. If the stakes are high, why would you not use all the time available to you to make your decision? In rushing ahead you squander the most elemental resource available to each of us—time. When confronted by high stakes concerns harvest all available relevant information, garner the opinions of those you trust, reflect upon the problem, take some time to think over options, communicate effectively, and use the time you have. Impulsive decisions can work out. They can also lead to disasters otherwise avoided. Finishing first is not the goal when making decisions. This is not a race to be won by the first person to soar across the decision-making finish line. Use time as a resource and cherish it. Sometimes, those few extra days or hours will be the difference between a terrible defeat and a reasonable success. Use time as an ally and not as an opponent.

# 81

## *"No personal significance, or insignificance, can spare one or another of us."*

I N THE END, WE ARE ALL MORTAL. THE ACCOMPLISHMENTS, problems, defeats, and achievements of our lives will fade to memory and dust. It is very easy for leaders to get caught up in the schimera of fame. It can feel very good to be the problem-solving savior of a situation. Our list of successes can trail out behind us like the robes of a great monarch. Resumes can grow and define us as people of power and skill. However, that is all transitory. Leaders who begin to believe their press clippings are deceiving themselves. No individual is more important than the system within which they labor. No person will remain as a fixture in their assignment forever. All things must pass. We deceive others and ourselves when we begin to think about the work we do as permanent. Life is, by definition, impermanent. Think of some material object that you treasure. Over time that object will fade, decompose, shatter, or in some other way change beyond recognition. In the same vein, so too will we. It is a terrible but common error to get caught up in the importance of what you do. Naturally, it is important for a leader to accept the value of what he or she does. Leaders who are unsure about the nature of their work cannot really inspire others. Such people are without the core values that are precursors to success. Perhaps time, experience, or the sad buffeting of life has dimmed the purpose of such people. Maybe they will resurrect their values and move ahead. But, regardless, the fact remains that if we get too caught up in the heavy importance of our work and ourselves we miss the point. Everything in life is important—not just our work. Take a minute and ponder this question—is your work the most important thing in your life? If you answer yes, then you had better re-think your response. Can work supercede family, faith, charity, and the world around us in importance? The answer to that question rests in your spirit and is one worthy of pondering.

# 82

## *"The fiery trial through which we pass, will light us down, in honor or dishonor, to the latest generation."*

OUR PRESENT ACTIONS WILL INFLUENCE THE WORLD IN WHICH our children, grandchildren, and generations beyond live in. Each generation is like a link in a chain stretching forwards and backwards. If we behave in a moral way we exert a tiny but important influence upon the manner in which that link will be forged. It is every person's responsibility to realize that their actions have consequences not only for themselves but for others as well. We are part of the history of our species and our planet. If we act in ways that despoil the world we punish not only us but all future generations as well. As a leader you have a responsibility within your firm to attempt to function in an ethical manner. The legacy you leave behind should be one marked by values such as responsibility, honesty, fairness, compassion, empathy, and environmental soundness. Times can be very challenging. Factors of fate, unforeseen circumstance, and chance can act as harmful agents in our lives. Yet, regardless of the circumstances you find yourself in you are capable of making choices. Those choices build across your life. They become the fabric of your life and shape its form. Years from now, when you look back at the contributions you have made, will you be satisfied with that product. If, in thinking about that moment, you feel doubt or misgivings the time to change your behavior is now. Each life is a fiery trial of sorts. In the end its value will be determined by the course of the journey. Reflect on this theme and make the necessary adjustments while you still have the time, resources, faculties, and opportunity to do so. Regrets are weights that can drag your spirit to the bottom of the lake. In thinking about our past we set the stage for a better present and a more durable future.

# 83

*"Both parties deprecated war; but one of them would make war rather than let the nation survive; and the other would accept war rather than let it perish. And the war came."*

IF YOU HAVE BEEN INVOLVED IN WAR YOU REALIZE THAT, EVEN victorious soldiers, carry the debris of battle in their spirits. War ravages lands, destroys crops, orphans children, murders the innocent, and mars all that it touches. In Lao Tzu's *Tao te Ching* it is noted, "Where armies pass, brambles grow." In the workplace war is recreated in the form of bitterness and acrimony. There are leaders who talk about going over the top, flanking opponents, launching a blitzkrieg, or using search and destroy methods. This type of language generally has no place in the workplace as it represents untold suffering and bespeaks an aggressiveness that usually results in damage. If you, as a leader, must fight the good fight, in pursuit of a worthy cause then so be it. But, it is far better to wage no battles when confronting a problem. One need not go to war to defeat a foe. There are strategies linked to negotiation, conflict resolution, communication, and bargaining that can supercede the need to fight a war. The greatest generals realized that constant fighting could exact worse damage on their forces than their opponents. No army can wage perpetual war. Therefore, before sending out the troops, stop and think about more meditative strategies that could be used. Once the dogs of war are unleashed the cost will be far different than what was anticipated. No one can predict war's outcome. What can be predicted is that it will mar relationships, exact a human cost, and create destruction. Are you so certain that the cause you are advocating is worth those price tags? If not, then re-think your position and find an alternative that might work. If so, then still re-think what you are doing and do so in the cold light of reality and not some fanciful image of war's cost.

# 84

## *"Let us judge not that we be not judged."*

IN THE NEW TESTAMENT JESUS CONFRONTS A CROWD PREPARED to stone an alleged sinner to death. In looking at this scene Christ enjoins the crowd by stating, "Let he who is without sin cast the first stone." In thinking about these words no individual in the crowd can find the certitude to cast a stone. The sinner is released and a lesson has been delivered. It is easy to judge others. It is very difficult to objectively assess ourselves. If you are a leader who manages by example or exception you probably spend a great deal of time looking for & finding the weaknesses of others. Each of us has our foibles. None of us is immaculate in form, shape, demeanor, or spirit. Yet, despite the universally flawed nature of all life, there continue to be leaders who go through their daily lives ferreting out the weaknesses, mistakes, and insecurities of others. In fact, there must be many such leaders or the word "boss" would not have the negative connotation that it sometimes bears. If you would expect mercy when you have failed you must reach out with mercy to others in their times of trial. Judging is a part of leading. Evaluation of programs and staff is a natural responsibility for a leader. But evaluation need not be merciless in its nature. When you are evaluating a person's performance you are not judging their personhood. If you find yourself falling into a pattern of always finding things wrong with people it is time to stop and think about your leadership style. Leaders who are faultfinders will have few supporters. It is a supreme egotist who believes only they are right while others are wrong. If you hope to have a productive leadership career you will need to overcome any tendency to be a constant judge of others. Always think about how you would wish to be treated. Do you believe that you should always be judged, micromanaged, and treated like a child? If not, then why would you treat others in this fashion?

# 85

## *"You must remember that some things legally right are not morally right."*

I T IS EASY TO KNOW THE RULES, PROTOCOLS, PROCEDURES, AND regulations that apply to your area of supervision. All it requires to be proficient in the realm of legalities is to study the law as it relates to the field you are in. There are numerous workshops & seminars offered annually for leaders who wish to stay abreast of the changing nature of policies and legislation. Professional journals often deal with topics of this nature. Networking with experienced leaders can also enhance your proficiency in this area. It is essential to know what is legal and what is not in your area of responsibility. One of the cardinal errors that a leader can make is to assume that what he or she is doing is legally kosher and then find out they are wrong. Litigation is expensive when you win the case, and potentially devastating if you lose. It is far better to know the law and avoid litigious entanglements. Further, the letter of the law may allow people to do things that would be seen by the vast majority of honest people as corrupt. The law allows people to devastate the environment and receive tax benefits for doing so. Laws make it permissible for obviously, and in some cases self-proclaimed, guilty parties to go free due to a failure to afford some arcane legal right to them prior to trial. What is legally permissible is generally what is ethical as well. Laws evolve over time to reflect the moral nature of the cultures they grow from. Therefore, laws should represent a society's best effort to be equitable, just, and decent. Yet, during their careers most leaders will confront circumstances wherein what is deemed "legal" strikes them as "immoral." An example of this might be having the right to dock a fine person's pay, or even terminate them, for making a mistake that was uncharacteristic. Of course, you could fire a person in such a situation. But, would that draconian action be truly fair and earnest? If you see shades of gray in such a situation take some time and reflect on the facts of the case. We are all imperfect beings. Every single one of us has made, and will continue to make, mistakes. Use judgment when you can and do not simply rely upon the utterly strict interpretation of vague points of law. Certainly, an ethical leader will not commit violations of law or code that are egregious. However, only a robotic leader will look at the words on the page of a legal code and mechanically apply them to every situation regardless of the human cost involved. You cannot lead if all you do is woodenly recite the regulations. You must know them but use your heart as well as the musty regulatory manuals and policy books that sit on the shelf in your office.

# 86

## *"Truth is generally the best vindication against slander."*

**I**F YOU LEAD, PEOPLE WILL CRITICIZE YOU. SOME OF THE criticism will be just as we are all made of the same imperfect clay. Other critiques will be unfair or based upon faulty information. In those situations the natural course of events, or effective communication on your part to team members, should help ameliorate the circumstances. However, in some situations the criticism aimed your way is premeditated & mean spirited. Leaders are often slandered or vilified in unethical ways. One need only think of political campaigns where issues linked to a candidate's alleged adulterous relations, past alcohol use, wartime cowardice, or mental health have all been intentionally twisted and misused to advance another person's agenda. Slander is an ugly thing. It bespeaks an immorality of action that is base. Slander is an overt example of the hatred that can drive people to behave in antisocial ways. In a very real sense such behavior is the equivalent of psychological violence. If you have had the experience of being slandered or libeled you may realize what a violation that is. In the face of such action you must rely upon truth as your greatest defense. In many cases lies can be overwhelmed by the cutting edge of truth's sword. If you are unable to respond to the vile attacks due to confidentiality factors, then be sure that you stress the consistently ethical pattern of behavior you have demonstrated over time. People who libel others generally have a history of unpleasantness. If you are a respected leader people will weigh your history against that of the slanderer and come to their own conclusions. If parties not bound by confidentiality are privy to the facts, encourage them to contact informal leaders in your team and set things straight. If you are free to speak—do so. But, in your rebuttals, be sure to take the high road and avoid being seen as too angry. It is permissible to let people know when you are hurt or wounded. The sharing of reasonable emotion is a human action that people will understand. However, if you go on the attack, people may well see both you and your false accuser as no different than politicians who regularly launch bitter smear campaigns rather than addressing issues. Simply state the facts as they are. Stress your past record. Avoid personally attacking your opponent. Move the conversation away form the incident and on to important initiatives or projects that are upcoming. Be as magnanimous as you can but never forget the nature of the situation. Once you know someone is capable of such base behavior always be aware of their actions. If possible, remove that person from your team as they are poisonous and will probably not repent or change. Do not believe their effusive apologies and judge them fairly based on their future and past behavior.

# 87

## *"I must run the machine as I find it."*

ONE OF THE WORST MISTAKES A LEADER CAN MAKE IS TO INITIATE massive changes in a system before he or she has taken the time to understand the way things work. Too many leaders come on board in new jobs and willy-nilly implement the processes, structures, and changes they want to see in place in a time span that is way too brief. People often fear and resist change. This is a futile pattern of behavior because change occurs around and within us all the time. But, it is important for leaders to realize the fears that are instilled in folks when they begin to hear about change agents, restructuring, and new brooms sweeping in various ways. Therefore, prior to instituting your agenda make sure that it fits into the culture you work in. In carefully assessing the people and systems in place within your organization you may come to realize that your previous game plan was mistaken. Only the most dysfunctional system requires a 100% alteration. By and large some good things are occurring in most places. Build on these positive attributes and augment them with reasonable and pragmatic changes over time. Run the machine you have been given and, when the time is right, fine-tune what needs to be modified. In my own work experience I remember once after a new superintendent was hired in the school district I was then employed by, I then experienced the sweeping sword of helter-skelter change. This individual had many years experience as a superintendent. He gave evidence of intelligence and an understanding of the need to assess before making changes. Yet, this party's declarations related to reasonable change were mere lip service. The new superintendent took one year to completely cull the administrative ranks, alter basic practices at the secondary level, implement vastly modified procedures in special education, and drive out some very good people without any deep understanding of the district's culture. The result of this approach

**129**

to change was disastrous and hurtful. Do not replicate this type of behavior. Get to know the people you work with and then make changes that are based upon knowledge rather than your own narrow preferences.

# 88

## *"Fearlessness for the right is a better thing than fearfulness for peace."*

SOMETIMES THERE IS A GREAT TEMPTATION TO TAKE THE EASY way out. Some problems arise that are so daunting that you may wish to simply ignore them and walk away. I have been in leadership situations when I tossed and turned at night repeatedly asking someone to please lift this burden from my shoulders. Sadly, being a leader will bring you to these types of moral crossroads. Very few people relish public humiliation, endless debate, or being hated. Yet, there are some battles that have to be fought regardless of the possible acrimony. If a person cannot stand up for basic ethical principles or decent causes because it will be hard—then they are not fit to lead others. If that is typical of your own pattern of behavior stop and reconsider any aspirations you have to be a leader. Great leaders have the capacity to fight for what is clearly right despite the odds. Many times their own desire to succeed in a good cause helps that very cause to prevail. Peace is the ultimate goal of almost everyone. But, in times of decision, you cannot balk at doing what is right simply because it will be challenging. Maintain your courage and fight for what is right. The alternative is to walk away and diminish both yourself and the world around you.

# 89

## *"Shades of opinion may be sincerely entertained by honest and truthful men."*

**I**T HAS BEEN MY MISFORTUNE TO WORK FOR SOME DICTATORIAL leaders. Such tyrannical figures brooked no opposition. If you disagreed with them they eventually recovered their pound of flesh from you in some cruel way. Tyrannical leaders are narcissists. They see their own needs, opinions, and values as the only acceptable ones. In their myopic view of the world all people who disagree with them are enemies to be suppressed. Reasonable debate or the expression of legitimate doubt are interpreted as rebellion, subversion, and animus. Such "leaders" make life miserable for many people who otherwise might shine & be effective. The world is generally not a "black & white" environment. Very few situations will come your way where there are no shades of gray built into the circumstances. Men and women who function as leaders need to accept and even embrace cultures within which people feel free to express reasonable opinions on any question. Through the synergy that occurs when multiple voices seek to answer a question comes a far stronger world than that created via dictatorship. One need only think of the drab and bitter existence that was spawned by dictators such as Hitler, Stalin, and Mao to realize that democratic institutions are necessary to prosper. Stop and think about your own experiences. It is very unlikely that you will be able to conjure up a dictator that crossed your path and feel anything but relief that he or she is now no longer a part of your life.

# 90

## *"The occasion is piled high with difficulty."*

L INCOLN MUST HAVE UTTERED THESE WORDS EITHER VERBALLY or within his mind many times during the tumultuous years of the Civil War. During his presidency Lincoln was bombarded with dire news, inter-personal malevolence, thousands of corrupt favor seekers, hundreds of thousands of deaths, and the rending of the nation. There must have been times when his confidence was shaken. Indeed, just prior to the presidential election of 1864 Lincoln called his cabinet together and spoke to them about the probability of his own electoral defeat. Still, despite all of the vicissitudes that Abraham Lincoln faced in his life as a leader he was able to overcome these, at times, catastrophic challenges. How did Lincoln maintain his equilibrium in the face of such pressure? Mr. Lincoln relied upon his pragmatic and analytical mind to reflect on events and develop flexible and strategic approaches. Lincoln appointed cabinet ministers who either possessed great acumen or whose appointment guaranteed the loyalty of important groups. In terms of generals, Lincoln was forced to use the tools he had until the forge of war determined who was ready to cut the ties of defeat and who was simply unable to bear the heat of forging. Abraham Lincoln rarely lost sight of his role as a servant and the fact that all of his decisions had consequences for the people of the nation. In following these types of pathways a leader can emulate Mr. Lincoln and overcome seemingly impossible odds. Leaders are called upon to deal with exceedingly difficult matters. How they perform in these tough situations will define not only their style but also the reputation that they earn.

# 91

## *"It is best not to swap horses while crossing the stream."*

THERE ARE OCCASIONS WHEN YOU WILL HAVE TO MAKE DIFFICULT personnel moves. Most people that you will work with are competent. Some colleagues are outstanding in their ability to accomplish things that need to be done. A select few are masters of their craft. These shining stars have the artistry and capacity to bring out the best in others and themselves. However, there are also people who are ill suited for the work that they do. If a leader wishes to succeed and help move his or her organization toward the path of excellence, they will need to first find out who these less capable people are and then deal with them. First, it is necessary to be sure, via careful evaluation, that a person is indeed incapable. Then it is ethical and necessary to afford this individual specific corrective feedback and opportunities to improve. Finally, if improvement has not been sufficient or noted, a change must be made. This is not a simple process. It is also not a process based upon ill will or vindictiveness. Another important element of this human resources issue is to realize that in most cases "nobody" is worse than "somebody." Lincoln's reference above was made after forceful politicians pushed him to make leadership changes in the midst of critical events. While Mr. Lincoln did make major personal moves at critical times, such as the replacement of General Joe Hooker as commander of the Army of the Potomac just days prior to the cataclysmic battle at Gettysburg, it was not his preferred mode of operation. If you constantly shake up the apple cart you will eventually end up with applesauce. Too much radical change will destabilize a system. Therefore, wait until the moment is right and then make the changes in personnel you see as appropriate at a time that best suits both the people involved and the work to be done. Swapping horses in midstream can be accomplished. But, such an exchange can also result in disaster and even drowning.

# 92

## *"Are you not over cautious when you assume that you cannot do what the enemy is constantly doing?"*

ABRAHAM LINCOLN PENNED THESE WORDS FOR THE BENEFIT OF one of the more irritating people he had to supervise. That man was Major General George Brinton McClellan.

McClellan was a relatively young commander who rose to national prominence in short order. Blessed with tremendous organizational skills, McClellan was a master at training and logistics. What McClellan lacked was the ability to act in a decisive manner, maintain reasonable perspective regarding the dangers he faced, accept criticism, or take any sort of risks. Due to these shortcomings McClellan fought battles that should have resulted in smashing victories but actually ended in stalemate or withdrawal. It could justly be said that McClellan's failures as a leader extended the Civil War by years and cost hundreds of thousands of lives. If you are in a leadership position and are confronted with difficult tasks you will gain little favor from either those who you supervise or those to whom you report if all you do is catalog the reasons why things cannot be accomplished. As a leader you must model a "can do" attitude. Emphasize the possibilities in a situation and not the gloom and doom. Few people will appreciate a leader who begins a campaign by expressing his or her certainty that the job cannot be done. Further, that sort of "leadership" probably will not endear you with your boss and will have some impact upon your longevity. Tersely put, either at least try to make a reasonable effort at succeeding or step aside and let someone else take the reins. In the end Lincoln fired General McClellan and then defeated him in the presidential election of 1864. To the end of his life McClellan never understood his shortcomings. He lived in a fantasyland of false accomplishment and unrealistic excuses. Avoid this miasma and take charge of the tough situations that will confront you as a leader. Do not make excuses and achieve results or someone else will do so in your absence.

# *"Why should there not be patient confidence in the ultimate justice of the people? Is there any better or equal hope in the world?"*

ALL TOO OFTEN NEW LEADERS WILL COME INTO A SYSTEM AND attempt to sweep everything clear. Such "change agents" commit a cardinal sin when they fail to take heed of the valuable experience that exists within the hearts and minds of many of the members of the new system within which this sort of pell-mell action takes place. Lessons of the past have value. History is a discipline that has great benefit. In learning what has worked and not worked over the years in a given organization a leader can plot out the likelihood of success with a much more reasonable sense than by simply shooting in the dark. Everything done in the past need not continue. One of the lessons that history teaches us is that people may well continue down pathways that lead to failure simply out of habit. A good question that a new leader can ask his or her staff is, "Why do we do things this way?" The answers to this question may shed light on the reasonableness of certain processes. However, in some instances the answer may well simply be, "Because we always have done it that way." In those situations it is reasonable to investigate whether or not what always has been done is what should be done in the future. Learn form the lessons that experience has taught both you and those around you. To turn a blind eye to the lessons of experience is to cripple your efforts. Such a self-inflicted wound is completely unnecessary. Why would you sacrifice the vital lessons of the past when they can steer you in the right directions? Only a person so full of pride and a sense of omniscience that they cannot even contemplate the value of other people's ideas could sacrifice such a valuable learning tool. Seek out your system's "historians" and listen to them. Then synthesize what you have learned and apply the teachings to the future. In this way you develop a leadership process that has a continuum of practice involving past, present, and future directions. The alternative is to re-invent your organization's culture from scratch and that is an endeavor that you will not be able to do.

## 94

*"I am a firm believer in the people. If given the truth, they can be depended upon to meet any national crisis. The great point is to bring them the real facts."*

P EOPLE WILL RESPOND BETTER TO TRUTH THAN TO SUBTERFUGE. In times of crisis most people would rather know the facts than to be misled. Faced with the reality of crisis people can at least have some chance to cope with it. If crisis descends upon people unprepared for it the results can be far worse than anyone can imagine. If you are a leader who must deal with a crisis have sound information and share it with the people involved. Then use the human and material resources available to meet the crisis. Involve people with the greatest expertise in planning, implementing, and evaluating an intervention plan designed to best cope with the crisis. How can you accomplish any of these vital tasks in an environment where lies replace facts? Leaders will be most closely scrutinized at crisis points. It is in those most difficult circumstances that people's vital interests, or their very lives, are at risk. In such situations a leader must be brave and honest. He or she cannot hide failures or disguise shortcomings with fancy rhetoric or slick excuses. In times of crisis leaders must harness the abilities of everyone involved. In order to accomplish that potentially life saving result a leader must tirelessly strive to keep people informed and mobilize resources. People are amazingly resilient. They can overcome tremendous odds. Think about disasters both natural and manmade that have occurred over the millennia. In Mr. Lincoln's time America stood as a divided nation. Armies swept across the land devastating the towns and fields through which they passed. Battlefield failures left Abraham Lincoln's government facing the reality of potential defeat. Millions of African-Americans remained in cruel bondage. If ever there was a crisis in American history it was the Civil War that hung over Mr. Lincoln's presidency like a blood red cloud. Yet, that war was won. Although Lincoln did not live to see the successful conclusion of the war, his leadership was a major factor in the achievement of that important result. In a crisis a leader must come through or they really are not fit to lead.

# 95

## *"We must extinguish our resentment if we expect harmony and union."*

THERE ARE LEADERS WHO TIRELESSLY SEEK OUT THE SMALLEST mistakes that people make and draw attention to them. Other leaders will look at a successful project and see only the two or three areas for improvement that can be noted. This is akin to a parent who takes a child's spelling test and says, "Oh, you got a 95%. It's too bad you missed that one word. You'll have to do better next time." This sort of "management by exception" approach will swiftly demoralize a child or a system. No one wants to be criticized for picayunish reasons. Accepting criticism requires a mature mind. It is hard to acknowledge shortcomings. It is doubly hard to do so if the feedback you are receiving is petty. Behavioral research teaches us that the most powerful force we have to modify behavior is sincere positive reinforcement. A leader will get much more mileage out of praise that punishment. Praise needs to be linked to actual achievement or improvement. People will catch on to hollow praise. One can only receive a few pats on the back for tasks that are routine or not even very well done before it becomes clear that the praiser is either insincere or ignorant. Likewise, it only takes a few harsh words to build barriers as strong as the former Berlin Wall. People have long memories. If you hurt them they will recall it and hold it against you for quite a while. Therefore, be positive in your demeanor, link praise to achievement or improvement, restrain yourself from nit picking, and only criticize when it is necessary to achieve necessary results. Think back to your own experience as a subordinate. Did you ever work for a "leader" who looked over your shoulder with a harshly critical eye? Were you ever taken to task for your performance in a way that rankled you? If so, then do not behave that way toward others.

# 96

## *"The probability that we may fail in the struggle ought not to deter us from the support of a cause we believe to be great."*

IF YOU ARE VERY FORTUNATE IN YOUR LIFE YOU MAY BE CALLED upon to be involved in a great cause. If you are doubly fortunate you may be asked to take a leadership role in such a worthy cause. In many instances the greatest causes begin as seemingly hopeless ventures. Did many people in the South really believe that civil rights would become a reality in a world that had been dominated by whites for so many decades? At the height of the Nazi war machine did it seem reasonable to believe that Hitler's legions would be utterly defeated? In Mr. Lincoln's day would it have seemed probable that the Union Army would emerge victorious after the terrible defeats of the first two years of war? In each of these instances, and countless others across the pantheon of human history, underdogs emerged victorious. Those results would never have been achieved if only faint-hearted folks were in charge of the endeavors. Great causes still exist and cry out for leadership support. In a world where violence and brutality can overwhelm the common folk there are still people who involve themselves in human rights causes, environmental pursuits, prison reform missions, and peace advocacy. If you want to achieve fulfillment not only of your own ego but also by helping others for generations, find your niche in such a cause. Then apply the great capacities that you possess to slowly moving forward a prosocial agenda that might otherwise falter without the support of decent people. There are "tipping points" in human history. Times where ideas once seen as remote or even harebrained emerge as the accepted status quo. For example, it would be hard to imagine a world where "whites only" and "colored only" signs would commonly grace water fountains, restrooms, and other public commodes. Yet, that world existed only a few decades ago in America. Be part of the movement toward a "tipping point" in some arena that you believe in and help make the world a more humane place now and in the future.

# 97

*"If we cannot give freedom to every creature,
let us do nothing that will impose slavery upon
any other creature."*

IN SOME SITUATIONS THE BEST THING A LEADER CAN DO IS
simply not make things worse. There are occasions when the
desired agenda cannot be implemented. In such circumstances an
effective leader first realizes that it is time to make a strategic
withdrawal. Then, in that withdrawal or retrenchment process, he
or she must make every effort to not damage things that already
have been built. For example, if a school principal has, with his
or her staff, set a goal for improving reading scores by 5% as per
state assessments and the test results indicate a 0% gain, analysis
needs to occur. However, that analysis need not include a
battering ram that destroys not only the palace gate but large
segments of the outer wall as well. In looking at results that are
less than expected a leader can also point toward ways in which
people have done well. Then through a pooling of human and
material resources the team can assess what needs to be done and
how. An underachievement of results can be a springboard for
analysis and future improvement. Success is not continual.
Human beings are imperfect creatures. If you expect continuous
growth of an exponential nature you will be disappointed. When
you cannot or did not accomplish your goals, step back and try to
figure out why that was the case. Do not make things worse by
either lashing out or ignoring deficits. Try to acknowledge where
you are, figure out where you are going, and do not drive off the
road because you are looking at the roadmap of "failure" that you
have in hand.

# 98

*If once you forfeit the confidence of your fellow citizens, you can never regain their respect and esteem."*

**T**RUST LOST IS DIFFICULT TO REGAIN. REPUTATION ONCE tarnished is difficult to re-polish.

There are times when you, as a leader, will be unable to share information or details with others. For example, you cannot discuss employee personnel or disciplinary matters with other parties. No matter how many times an interested party asks you about such a personnel matter, you will be unable to answer them. However, overt lying is never a good practice. Liars can prevail in some circumstances and for a limited amount of time. They cannot build a culture of trust or engender the long-term respect of colleagues. In fact, a leader whose word is doubted cannot be respected regardless of how capable they may be in other aspects of their work. Sometimes leaders make false claims & promises in order to win over people. This approach will not be a winning one. People may appear naïve but they really are not. Therefore, make it a cardinal rule not to lie or mislead. If you can at least be honest people will have some level of respect for you. If not, all you will receive is false support and distrust.

# 99

## *"Beware of rashness, but with energy and sleepless vigilance go forward and give us victories."*

PRESIDENT LINCOLN DIRECTED THESE WORDS TO GENERAL Joseph Hooker upon his appointment of him as Commander-In-Chief of the Army of the Potomac. Hooker was an ambitious and egotistical man. He had actively campaigned to both undermine his predecessor in this assignment, General Ambrose Burnside, and win his job. Hooker had also been heard to utter some brash talk about the nation needing a dictator of whom he was just the man for the job. Lincoln appointed Hooker to the role of commander of the Union's largest army despite these factors, all of which he was aware of. However, Lincoln wrote to Hooker to let him know both his expectations and his knowledge of Hooker's character. In the end Hooker was unsuccessful as an army commander and Lincoln continued his search for generals capable of winning the war. In this enjoinder Lincoln combined two complementary but seemingly contradictory factors. Great leaders instinctively know that rash action is risky. A rash leader can achieve great victories. They can also be utterly crushed due to their innate inexpedience. There is a great difference between a bold commander and one who leaps into the abyss with no forethought. General Grant was a bold commander who ultimately engineered the defeat of the Confederacy. General Custer was a rash leader who ended up dead with his entire command on a dry field in Montana in 1876. The goal of all leaders must be the accomplishment of the tasks they are charged with. Those victories can take as many forms as there are enterprises under the sun. The finest leaders know the value of action as well as that of planning. Most victories are won before the first actions are taken. Once action begins then all energy must be directed to the accomplishment of the goals. Beware of rashness but move on in a concerted way to accomplish the necessary victories you need to move ahead along with your organization.

# 100

*"Well, a ruler once asked his advisors if there was one maxim that could be truly applied in all times and situations. The advisors returned and presented him the words: 'And the, too, shall pass away.' How much it expresses. How chastening to the hour of pride. How consoling in the depths of affliction."*

IN OUR LIVES THERE ARE TIMES OF GREAT JOY AND BITING sadness. These high and low points sometimes seem like they will never end. We are tested by life's changing circumstances. Think back to some of the saddest moments in your life. Perhaps the death of a loved one haunts you. There may be some career defeats that still send a chill up your spine. Maybe you fell prey to the depths of depression and questioned the very reason for your life. Life can embrace or consume us. In leadership there will be periods in your career when you feel the overwhelming loneliness and pain that can be part of this difficult field. Such epochs in your life may seem perpetual. In reality, those are but segments of your life. The hard times, like all portions of your life, will pass along. Our lives move in a cyclical rhythm of ups and downs. Periods of it are calm while others are not. Regardless of the powerful feeling tone of any event or age in a person's life, all things must pass. If you sit quietly and think back to five years ago, it may be difficult to specifically remember what were the most important work related issues in your life. The issues that stare us in the face today with seemingly infinite importance may be difficult to even recall in a few months or years. Maintaining a balanced perspective is a survival skill for any leader. What leaders do is important but transitory. Even the greatest leaders in human history will pass on into oblivion. Do the best that you can with every day that is given to you. Count each day as a blessing and make positive use of it. When times are rocky remember Mr. Lincoln's realism and let those harsh moments pass on. Learn from them and let them go.

# Postscript

*In closing I offer you the following two simple verses to reflect on when you think about your own leadership style and the way in which you affect those people who work around you.*

### An American Boss
Ramrod straight at the table's head he sits.
A rap of his gold-ringed knuckle on the wood underscores his point.
Monogrammed cuffs peak out from a silken sleeve.
His shirt as white as a Donner Party blizzard.
A tie of elegant design rests against a striking vest.

Encased in a designer suit he plows along.
Speaking without listening—ruling but not leading.
A suit without a soul—fabric standing in for substance.
A true image of the American boss.

### Loyalty
For years I strove to do my work.
Service is a concept of value.
In helping others, we help ourselves as well.
If our daily path can cross another's and be of aide we have served that day.
Yet, the powers-that-be often search for mere control.
Such "power" is a soul-drying construct.
It seeps into every pore and leaves a spiritual skeleton where a full-blooded person should reside.
Past services appear as nothing as the new broom sweeps all before it.
What was in place is, by its very history, adjudged as wrong.

Old ways, no matter how sensible, must be deconstructed and
altered.
Results are not really the issue—what matters is the leader's
focus and ability to make a change occur.
Like a czar ordering the peasants off their land, the leader forges
ahead.
Old soldiers fall by the wayside—victims of the new tactics and
strategy.
Their loss is but the common cost of new ideas.
What often follows is chaos, but that matters little.
What is important is the leader's unrelenting will and its
satisfaction.
Eventually, the leader moves on to new opportunities.
A "change agent" with a growing resume as impressive as a
manuscript illuminated by a medieval monk.
What remain are the ruins.
Over time, and if repeated, such actions sap the spirit of the
system.
Loyalty to people is a just course.
To be loyal to institutions or rank is a fool's errand.
When we offer loyalty, we extend our trust and hope.
Snuffed out enough times, those traits are ground to dust.
How sad when a leader's footprint helps grind our vocational
soul into the ground.
Such actions can reduce the spirit of a system to dust in the wind.
If you lead, bear in mind the trust given to you.
In leading well there is hope.
In leading with compassion there is justice.
In leading with others there is consensus.
If you place ego and power above these traits you do not lead.
Instead you create the dogma of defeat that substitutes control for
consequence.
Learn the lesson of the ages.
He or she who will lead must serve as well.
Therein lies the secret of loyalty earned and lost.

GMR/2006

# Suggested Reading

Davis, William C., *Lincoln's Men: How President Lincoln Became Father to and Army and a Nation,* New York, NY: The Free Press, 1999.

Donald, David Herbert, *Lincoln,* New York, NY: Simon & Schuster, 1995

Donald, David Herbert, *"We Are Lincoln Men": Abraham Lincoln and His Friends,* New York, NY: Simon & Schuster, 2003

Griessman, Gene, *Words Lincoln Lived By: 52 Timeless Principles to Light Your Path,* New York, NY: Fireside, 1997

Humes, James C., *The Wit & Wisdom of Abraham Lincoln,* New York, NY: Gramercy Books, 1996.

Leidner, Gordon, *A Commitment to Honor: A Unique Portrait of Abraham Lincoln in His Own Words,* Nashville, TN: Rutledge Hill Press, 2000

Stone, Tanya Lee, *Abraham Lincoln: A Photographic Story of a Life,* New York, NY: DK Publishing, 2005

www.ingramcontent.com/pod-product-compliance
Lightning Source LLC
LaVergne TN
LVHW011235080426
835509LV00005B/514